Ready, Steady, Retire!

Plan Your Way to Success in a Redefined Retirement

Justin King

Martin Bamford

Ready, Steady, Retire!

Plan Your Way to Success in a Redefined Retirement

Justin King and Martin Bamford

Foreword by Jill Insley

First edition published in Great Britain 2014

Copyright © 2014 by Justin King and Martin Bamford

The rights of Justin King and Martin Bamford to be identified as the authors of this work have been asserted by them in accordance with the Copyright, Designs and Patents Act 1998.

ISBN: 978-1-326-05651-3

Typeset in Bell MT

MFP Wealth Management
88 Mudeford,
Christchurch,
Dorset, BH234AS
www.mfpwealthmanagement.co.uk

Informed Choice Chartered Financial Planners
Sundial House, 20 High Street,
Cranleigh,
Surrey, GU6 8AE
www.icfp.co.uk

Contents

About the Authors

Justin King

Justin is a Chartered Financial Planner and Certified Financial Planner, passionate about retirees living a rewarding and successful retirement.

He is Managing Director of MFP Wealth Management, an award-winning family firm of Chartered Financial Planners in the retirement capital of the UK, Christchurch in Dorset.

When not helping clients plan their "perfect retirement", Justin enjoys sailing, windsurfing and spending time with his partner Kathy and their two daughters.

Martin Bamford

Martin is a Chartered Financial Planner and Certified Financial Planner. He is Managing Director of Informed Choice, an award-winning firm of Chartered Financial Planners in Cranleigh, Surrey.

His main focus is care fees planning for vulnerable clients and he is well versed in the various issues faced by individuals as they enter residential care.

Outside of work, Martin is father to three young children and partner to Becky, a primary school teacher. He is a keen runner, participating in marathon and ultra-distance races.

Foreword

Baby boomers are considered by some - mainly by those who are not baby boomers - to have it all.

The head of insurance giant Legal & General, Nigel Wilson, recently sparked controversy by arguing that baby boomers - the 14 million people who were born in the UK during the post-World War II baby boom between 1946 and 1964 - had effectively "lived for free".

The capital gains they have made on their homes have far outweighed the cost of mortgage payments, meaning they have effectively paid nothing for accommodation. They have also benefited from free healthcare thanks to the NHS, support from the welfare state, and free education.

No student loans or tuition fees for them, he pointed out.

Many of the oldest members of this generation are already reaping the benefits of a well provided-for retirement. Some have even benefited from the gold standard in pensions - the final salary scheme.

Wilson points to inequality between baby boomers and those born after 1964: he does not identify any difference in fortune between those born early in the baby boom period and those coming later on. But not all those born in the post-War period have enjoyed the same benefits.

The so-called Generation Jones, a name used to describe those born between 1954 and 1965, grew up to face mass unemployment and deindustrialisation just as they were about to join the UK's workforce in the 1970s.

Better healthcare and nutrition has led to increased longevity. But this in turn has developed new problems for baby boomers.

Some have become part of the "sandwich generation", feeling under pressure to give financial help to their children for the likes of college funding, rent, house deposits, and to their parents, who may need assistance with funding long term care.

And for those aged 50 up to 65 who are in the run up to retirement, things could just be about to get even more complicated. After decades of tinkering with pension regulations, the Government has developed a radical new system for the way pension funds can be used.

The new rules could change the lives of millions of retirees - for the better or worse - and baby boomers are the first generation who will have to get to grips with these radical changes.

The new regime of "pension freedom" is designed to give those aged 55 and over improved access to the money they have saved throughout their working lives. The necessity to buy an annuity has finally been removed for everyone, not just the wealthy with large pension pots.

Instead, investors can withdraw a series of lump sums from their pension pots for whatever purpose they choose. The new rules even allow all the pension fund to be withdrawn in one go.

The prospect of this increased freedom has led to speculation that investors will squander the money intended to see them through their retirement on world cruises and new cars. The more likely outcome, according to a survey by Saga, is that retirees will give money to their children.

The research indicates that one in seven over-50s plan to cash in all or part of their pension, with 13% of those giving some or all the money to their children and another 4% planning to help out their grandchildren, be it a deposit for a first home or school fees.

Jane, aged 52, is already planning to use her entire tax-free lump sum to pay her daughter's university tuition fees. "I cannot bear the idea of her coming out of university laden with tens of thousands of pounds of debt," she says.

Regardless of whether pension money is spent on a Lamborghini or used for a more altruistic purpose, retirees could live to regret their decision. Most people have not saved enough into their pensions to enable them to use the money for any purpose other than generating a retirement income.

According to the OECD, retirees need 70% of their pre-retirement income to live comfortably after they stop working. But a report by Aviva in 2012 indicates that in the UK, the gap between that expectation and what they might actually get is nearly £10,000 a year.

Jane admits that although she has invested in various pensions since first starting work, she has favoured a comfortable standard of living over maximising her pension contributions.

"I have always contributed but never the full amount possible. Even now, when I should be concentrating on my retirement income, I'm planning on spending my pension on something else. Even though I can rationalise it because I know I am doing a very worthwhile thing for my daughter, I know that if I spend my tax free lump sum in this way, it will make things financially tight for me later on," she says.

So, if like Jane, your pension planning leaves quite a lot to be desired, can anything be done to improve your retirement prospects? Well, the fact you are reading this book is a very good start.

Ready, Steady, Retire! – Plan Your Way to Success in a Redefined Retirement will take you through the challenges you are likely to meet as you navigate through retirement, explaining ways you can deal successfully with them and setting out the options that are now open to you.

You may be pleasantly surprised at how much you can do to improve your situation, from easing your way happily into retirement and improving your income, to making sure your family is looked after and that you have a "good death".

But there's one thing you can't afford to do - wait.

If, like me, you are in your fifties or sixties, you could be around for another *30, 40* or even *50* years. It's time to get planning, to make sure the rest of your life is really worth living.

Jill Insley,
The Sunday Times Personal Finance and Consumer Columnist,
November 2014

Chapter One
Introduction

Introduction

Now, do I think the baby boomers are self-absorbed? I do". - P. J. O'Rourke

The end of the Second World War in 1945 brought with it a baby boom in many western countries. Nine months after the bombs stopped falling, as historian Landon Jones later described the event, "the cry of the baby was heard across the land." This surge in the birth rate lasted from 1946 through to 1964 in the UK.

Now, almost 70 years later and these Baby Boomers are entering the retirement phase of their lives, commencing and redefining their 'second act'.

The term 'Baby Boomer' is society's label for the cohort born in the post-war period and is incredibly polarising amongst those who fit the criteria, but it is a term that best describes this group of individuals who have played an enormous part in shaping society as we know it today.

Modern Britain has been indescribably changed by its post-war generations. A generation that shaped modern youth culture, Baby Boomers twisted and shouted, championed new social freedoms, and became part of a world with - perhaps for the first time in history - a true sense of optimism for the future; a man even walked on the Moon!

The same generation witnessed the crippling inflation of the 1970s, protested against oil and gas shortages, drove the first Mini Coopers, thought about impeaching Nixon, and cheered for the deregulation of the City of London.

The post-war generation's attitudes, expectations and sheer demographics have redefined every stage of modern life, and retirement will surely be no exception.

This cohort has enjoyed exceptional political, social and economic advantages that make them, arguably, the luckiest generation to date. Between 1946 and 1960, over 12 million children were born in the UK, representing a population increase of 26% during a period of fifteen years[1]

The sheer size and spending power of this new demographic gave rise to a music industry and youth culture recognising the identity of youth as a generation on an unprecedented scale.

As teenagers and youth, those now approaching retirement benefitted from free secondary education compulsorily introduced under the 1944 Education Act, then went on to benefit from free university education and more or less full employment.

Historically, this generation was the healthiest and wealthiest the world had seen to date, and among the first to grow up genuinely expecting the world to improve with time[2].

Perhaps best summing up this unique generation is a Demos report from 2003[3], which concluded that Baby Boomers 'have transformed every station they have passed through and show no sign of stopping.'

The Boomers' booming wealth

An economy moving from strength to strength has supported the post-war generation's rosy outlook. The sheer shift in demographics, supported by a surge in the number of working women, created a booming labour supply that increased economic output across Britain.

Wealthier than the generation before them, they bought affordable homes that have steadily and consistently gained in value - up to a 100% increase in real terms in some cases. Being able to buy property and benefit from tax relief on your mortgage would be unheard of today.

As Boomers bought new, larger homes for growing families or second homes to holiday in, house prices rose even further. The growth of property ownership in the UK has resulted in this generation being an incredibly asset-rich group of individuals.

Mortgage and property expert Andrew Montlake explained to *Ready, Steady, Retire!* how dramatically homeownership has risen since the end of the War.

In 1945, as the first Boomers were born, homeownership sat at around 40% and this continued to grow until the mid-1970s when the political parties took on the mantle of 'the Englishman's home is his castle'. Various schemes gave buyers a leg up onto the property ladder, culminating in Thatcher's 'Right To Buy' scheme which remained in force up until 2003, when property ownership peaked at around 70%.

Andrew explained that this vast increase was driven by a combination of massive deregulation, easily accessible credit and significantly wider mortgage availability than we see today. It cannot be underestimated how much the upsurge of wealth amongst today's retirees has been helped along by homeownership and substantial house price rises.

Collectively, more than 80% of the nation's £6.7 trillion wealth is owned by the post-war generation. Of the £2.6 trillion in shares or savings, Boomers own more than £1 trillion, as well as 40% of the £2.5 trillion tied up in property. This generation accounts for a third of Britain's £1.8 trillion in pension assets (and another 25% is held by individuals aged 45-50).

Having a home has proved such an astonishingly good investment that 1 in 5 Boomers now own a second home. They also own 80% of all top-of-the-range cars, go on 80% of cruises and buy 50% of skincare products[4].

Benefitting from the investment boom years of the 1980s, many of today's new retirees have worked hard and will be rewarded with the guaranteed income of a final salary pension. This, for many, will deliver the peace of mind in retirement they desire, without worrying about the ups and downs of the stock market.

With this hard-working ethic however, comes reluctance amongst many retirees to spend freely in later life - particularly for those without the security of a guaranteed income in retirement.

Booming health

Alongside improved financial stability, the Boom generation has revolutionised quality of life through tremendous advances in healthcare that will permanently alter the notion of retirement. Today's new retirees will live more than 30 years longer than their grandparents did - a whole second adult lifetime - due to advances in medicine[5].

Today, more people survive cancer than die from it. Common killers, including tuberculosis, measles and polio have been almost completely eradicated. The sequencing of the genome in 1952 gave rise to treatments for genetic conditions like haemophilia and cystic fibrosis that frequently caused early death.

Organ transplants and biotech once thought of as space age help failing bodies live longer, with healthy productive results.

Perhaps more importantly, treatment for chronic conditions and disabilities has improved immensely, granting an extraordinary new lease of life to older people.

Cataracts affect between five and ten per cent of the ageing population, forming cloudy patches on the lens of the eye that can lead to severely blurred or misty vision, making many simple tasks nearly impossible. With 90% of all patients successfully treated, The British Medical Association estimates that advances in modern cataract surgery can add as many as 30 years of high-quality life to an individual[6].

Alongside symptomatic relief, early intervention and medical treatment in a number of illnesses is credited with a dramatic increase in lifespan. The diagnosis and appropriate treatment of high blood pressure has had astonishing effect - incidences of heart attack and stroke are falling faster than any other medical phenomenon in the UK.

Buoyed by good health and strong personal finances, Boomers have led a revolt against common perceptions of ageing.

Where retirement literature of the 1950s encouraged "a quiet and suitably modest" existence[7], a quick look at a current local newspaper or supermarket notice board will reveal a plethora of options, from samba dancing to sushi-making, singing to Spanish.

People are travelling more frequently - The National Travel Survey finds adults over 60 make more trips, local, national, and international, than any other age group.

As a generation, Baby Boomers have staunchly retained their independence - as they have aged, they have spearheaded drives to stay in their homes and retain their driving licenses.

As the oldest of the Baby Boomers approach their seventies, Britain has been forced to radically rethink how they perceive the elderly and ageing, with a renewed focus on security and empowerment.

Ready, Steady, Retire!

Within this book we have condensed decades of our combined experience working with retiring and elderly clients to create a practical guide designed to help those approaching retirement today consider all of the issues.

In addition to the Financial Planning considerations for which the authors are best known, this book explores the lifestyle factors that retirees will need to think about and plan for over the next generation. This knowledge and experience has been supplemented with views from leading experts and real-life case studies, bringing examples of successful retirements to life.

In the next chapter we have set out the current state of the nation, as we see it for those retiring today and over the course of the next decade. These are the main social, demographic and lifestyle factors which we believe will influence important retirement decisions. Knowledge of these issues will help you plan for a successful retirement.

Chapter three describes how to retire successfully in the current climate. As Financial Planners we have worked with hundreds of clients to plan for and implement a successful retirement. This chapter takes lessons from successful retirements and shares them with readers.

In chapter four we consider the rise of the silver splitter. We examine rising rates of separation and divorce in retirement, looking at what can be done to maintain healthy relationships and thinking about the consequences of relationship breakdown in later life.

Chapter five examines the squeezed sandwich generation; those individuals or couples retiring today who also have to support elderly parents and adult children. Being squeezed between two generations places additional pressure on time and finances; something which has to be planned for when retiring.

Chapter six is all about the diseases which will define the post-war generation in retirement. With greater life expectancy for this generation comes a greater risk of suffering from dementia and other age-related diseases in later life. Our expert view within this chapter offers practical steps people of all ages can take today to avoid walking right into the dementia firing line.

In chapter seven we consider the toll of old age care. Improved life expectancy also means more people are spending at least some of their retirement in need of long-term care, delivered at home or in a residential care environment. Within this chapter we look at considerations for funding care and finding the right care solution in later life.

Chapter eight explores the taboo topic of death. We write about what it means to have a 'good death' and how planning for this final stage of life is such an important step for everyone to take in retirement. Our expert view in this chapter is an enlightening discussion about death with the founder of a natural burial site.

In chapter nine we explain how to create an effective plan for a successful retirement. We look at the Financial Planning process and identify how to find a suitable professional adviser to help you through this important planning process.

Thank you

We hope you enjoy reading this book and find its contents valuable. We do of course welcome your feedback and any questions you have.

You can contact Justin by email to jk@mfpwealthmanagement.co.uk or by calling 01425 279212. You can also talk to Justin on Twitter at @justinking_mfp.

You can get in touch with Martin by email to martin@icfp.co.uk or by phoning 01483 274566. Martin is on Twitter at @martinbamford.

Chapter Two
The State of the Nation

The State of the Nation

"One of the hallmarks of the Baby Boomer generation is that it doesn't live like the previous generation. It hasn't yet given up jeans and t-shirts or beer." - Ron Klugman

The post-war generation are experiencing mixed feelings about their future as they start planning for retirement.

Those in their fifties and sixties may be nervous about weathering recent economic storms which have battered some retirement plans. Investment returns have been volatile in recent years, annuity rates have tumbled, and mid-to-late generation Baby Boomers will see their company pensions scaled back.

The global financial crisis of 2007 and 2008 threw a spanner in the works for the leading edge of Baby Boomers as they reached retirement age, prompting as it did stock market falls and a prolonged period of low interest rates.

This surely is a financial storm of exceptional economic conditions during which to enter retirement.

So what will retirement look like for this generation of retirees?

Whilst those retiring today have a significantly longer life to look forward to, this longer life will require a substantially larger pot of money to fund it, and, for all of medicine's astronomical advances, that longer life may not necessarily be a healthy one.

With the average cost of care in the UK rapidly approaching £28,000 per year, the burden of costs weighs heavily on many a retiree's mind[8].

Many of the same generational advantages that so favoured the post-war generation have had unintended consequences for their families; many of this cohort are watching their children and grandchildren struggle with house prices, university fees, rising taxes and falling social services, and consequently they hope to be able to contribute financially, whilst often enough still caring for elderly parents. The phrase 'squeezed sandwich generation' has never been so relevant.

As a nation we are in a period of transition, from a society where we expected to be nurtured and, to an extent, provided for from the cradle to the grave, to one where we increasingly need to support ourselves.

Boomers are often experiencing this phenomenon for the first time as they reach retirement, having lived within a paternalistic state for most of their lives.

Increasingly, this generation will need to make more choices themselves, which may come as a culture shock for some who have been comfortable being provided for with free education, free healthcare, and healthy final salary pension schemes.

Having said that, their reputation for redefining the world around them at every stage of their lives will surely stand Boomers in a better position than many previous generations to deal with this challenge.

Retirement redefined

The post-war generation will retire unlike any generation before them, and their planning and financial needs will differ wildly from those of previous generations.

Consulting relatives or the Internet, Boomers may well feel that their vision of retirement is different or unusual. Quite simply, it is. No generation has retired this way before.

In the context of constant change, of major demographic movements and a revolution in expected longevity, the nature of retirement has shifted and will continue to shift in the future. Boomers, as they redefine retirement, will also drastically redefine retirement planning as they explore how to support retirement as it should be; a period of growth, security, and self-discovery.

The longevity revolution

The increase in longevity experienced by the Baby Boomer generation is nothing short of astonishing.

In the early part of the 20th century, a healthy man or woman could only reasonably expect to live into their early 50s. By the end of the Second World War in 1946, a 45-year old man might optimistically expect to live into his late 60s, whilst a 45-year old woman could reasonably hope to celebrate her 70th birthday.

By contrast, the peak generation of Baby Boomers had an average life expectancy of 76 years at birth, and advances in health sciences and medical care have improved the outlook even further; a 65-year old can, in the year 2014, realistically plan to live until their mid-80s[9].

Baby Boomers are living on average an astonishing 34 years longer than their grandparents did - an amazing increase in longevity that has radically redefined both their hopes and concerns for retirement.

As the Boomer generation plans for its later years, the opportunities before it seem apparently limitless. There will be plenty of time to travel, build close relationships with children and grandchildren, volunteer for social causes, give back to the community, and rediscover lost passions for art and creative enterprise.

Whilst longevity blesses this generation with a spectacularly long 'second act' in which to enjoy his or her life, it also brings financial and personal challenges that no previous generation has faced.

With a longer life comes an increasing probability of illness or disability in later retirement, and research supports the conclusion that our longer lives may not necessarily be healthier ones.

Nearly 80% of adults over 65 have at least one chronic condition requiring treatment, and 50% have two[10]. Among people aged 65 and over, 40% have some disability that limits their independence, and age-related degenerative diseases like Alzheimer's Disease remain incurable.

Even for the very healthy, the emotional and psychological burdens of supporting partners through such illness can be devastating, particularly as long-term health care grows steadily more expensive.

Nearly 8% of adults over 65 in the UK report feelings of anxiety and depression, connected most regularly with stresses caused by care obligations and financial insecurity[11].

The planning challenge

Among the more tangible challenges of our growing longevity is planning accurately for a sustainable and fulfilling retirement.

The combined forces of life expectancy increases and retirees' expectations of their retirements improving, offer plenty of time and opportunity to spend money. Even late in life when no longer spending on cruises, playing golf, or exploring foreign countries, adequate income is essential to support basic costs of living.

In 1965, most major UK banks advised customers save sufficiently to support a retirement period of fifteen years; today's retirees must plan for close to thirty years of living and healthcare costs.

As longevity increases, the traditional dream of retiring at age 65 may become unrealistic. The issues surrounding increasing life expectancy often force people to continue working and building their retirement pot for longer before they can enjoy the fruits of their labour in earnest.

Defined benefit or 'final salary' pensions were once the norm for many workers in the UK, offering the promise of an inflation-linked retirement income for life.

Many of the first wave of Baby Boomers, now already enjoying or approaching retirement, are fortunate enough to benefit from these schemes, but for those who don't, planning adequately for an income through retirement remains challenging.

Without a genuine understanding of your projected retirement income based on pension provision or a consolidated pension strategy with a clear end goal, the apparently endless number of calculations involved in understanding options for retirement can be an impossible challenge.

Maintaining real value

Longevity exposes an often under-considered problem in retirement planning. Price inflation can hugely reduce the buying power of a fixed income in retirement, a detriment of particular note to those planning to build their own pension pot.

For example, an item costing £100 to purchase today will cost £163 after a decade of inflation at 5% a year. After 30 years, that same good or service costing £100 would cost £432. The longer you live, the greater the impact of price inflation. Whilst seldom discussed, the inflation risk is probably the most significant risk you will face when it comes to providing an income which retains its spending power.

Furthermore, with interest rates on savings being at an almost historical low, many Boomers find themselves nervous about being able to fund retirement through to their 80s or 90s.

Previous generations were able to survive from their nest egg - the savings they had put aside - because interest rates were more favourable and life expectancy was shorter. Today's retirees look to their elderly parents and see the huge expense incurred for funding care and how their savings are being eaten up in paying for the care they need, whilst simultaneously being eroded by inflation.

With a large percentage of assets tied up in property, some members of this generation are finding themselves asset rich and cash poor, as savings are reduced year after year. For many there is a balance to strike between enjoying the early years, whilst still being able to afford care in later life, if it's needed.

Unsurprisingly, many retirees struggle to appreciate that they will, in all probability, live for another thirty years and as a result risk not planning sufficiently for the very real financial consequences. Only 15% of over 65s admit to always saving or investing in products which aim to achieve above-inflation returns, suggesting the awareness of the inflation risk is horrifyingly low[12].

What's more, the real rate of inflation experienced by retirees is often higher than the official rate of inflation, as they're not buying the latest consumable goods which help to drive down the published inflation rates. Instead they are spending their money on food, fuel and other goods which we typically see increasing in value rapidly.

Coupled with an unknown life expectancy, inflation risk is one of the biggest challenges facing Baby Boomers planning to fund the next 30 years of their lives.

Confidence in the future

As a generation, the retirees of today are relatively confident in their financial future, compared to the general population.

According to a study carried out by Mintel, 38% of British Boomers said they felt confident about their finances for the coming year, compared to just 28% of all adults[13]. The resurgence of the British economy following the credit crisis may explain some of the assuredness, alongside improving property values and return rates, and, perhaps equally importantly, increasing consumer confidence.

It is important to ensure this confidence is not misplaced. The transition to retirement can be complex, and taking time to understand all the financial demands of retirement is essential.

Some of that confidence may well arise from the Boomer's generational self-reliance and their unprecedented personal wealth. The net wealth of retired families is projected to rise over the next ten years[14].

The primary driver behind this trend is the growing earned income among 65- to 74-year-olds who continue to work in to retirement. A phased approach to retirement is increasingly common, with workers shifting to part-time or contract positions before leaving their careers permanently. Recent legislation in the UK has facilitated choosing to work beyond retirement age if desired.

Starting a business in retirement is also increasingly common. According to the Prince's Initiative for Mature Enterprise, there are currently 4.17 million self-employed workers in the UK, of which 42% (1.75 million) are over 50. That's up from 38% in 2008.

About 1.4 million of this self-employed group are between 50 and 64 years old, and 375,000 - almost 1 in 10 - are 65-plus[15].

Such initiatives can make a valuable contribution to a privately-funded pension pot, but require careful planning if they are to provide an essential and sustainable income.

The value of property

Many retirees today are fortunate enough to own a home, viewing it as an asset that will provide essential financial support in their old age, and indeed the strength of the UK housing market over a lifetime has made home ownership a wise investment choice.

As an asset though, property must be viewed with caution. Unlike an increase in wealth driven by liquid, spendable assets such as savings and investments, the vast majority of the post-war generation can attribute their financial stability to a booming property market, which may not be maintained in the long term.

It could be argued that our national obsession with property – an overwhelming desire to own property - has resulted in some members of this generation holding a disproportionate percentage of their wealth in property.

For some, property is seen as a viable alternative to a pension, which may not have seemed so attractive during the property boom years as did investing in another property. There is however a risk in holding most of your assets in one asset class, instead of spreading the risk across different asset classes such as shares, bonds, cash and commodities (for example oil, gas and gold).

Releasing the equity captured in your home may also be complicated. Although many are attached to the idea of a family home to pass on to children, the realities of rates and maintenance in a large house can prove too draining in the long term. In an emergency situation when a house needs to be sold quickly, tactfully planning to maximise the value of the asset is nearly impossible.

Is all equal?

In any discussion of the chances of a successful retirement, income inequality should not be overlooked. Economic outlooks vary wildly across income brackets, as income inequality amongst Britain's population over the age of 65 continues growing.

Incomes in the 90th percentile, representing the most affluent 10% of the population, are estimated to grow at nearly 3.3% per year in real terms. Incomes in the 10th percentile, the least wealthy ten per cent, look set to continue a more modest growth of just 0.6% per year.

Against a current inflation rate of 1.5%, according to the Consumer Price In-dex[16], it is quickly apparent how the poorer segment of retirees will become poorer over time.

Expert view

We spoke to Justin Urquhart Stewart, co-founder of Seven Investment Management (7IM) and one of the most recognisable and trusted market commentators in the media.

Ready, Steady, Retire!: Do you agree with the comment that Baby Boomers are a privileged generation?

Justin Urquhart Stewart: Right from the moment they were born, Baby Boomers have had a huge impact upon the economy. These children were the first in decades who didn't have to deal with a World War - the wars they had to deal with were minor in comparison.

The level of expenditure on these children was vast. The growth of the economy as the nation recovered from war was significant as money was pumped in to aid recovery, which gave these Boomers a booming labour market to enter.

They then found themselves benefitting from pension structures which weren't going to be affordable in the future - but they didn't know that - which resulted in many Boomers moving towards retirement looking forward to the best possible retirement levels and the longest period of retirement ever known.

So yes, whilst no group is homogeneous, in many senses I would say the Baby Boomers are a fortunate generation.

Ready, Steady, Retire!: How much of a contrast is this to their parents' generation?

Justin Urquhart Stewart: If you look at the previous generation they were very parsimonious with their money because they lived through the War and a whole period of austerity. They found themselves at retirement in a position where their pensions were set, healthcare was set, and death was almost set shortly after retirement. Everything was preordained for them in many cases.

The culture of individuality of the 60s and 70s means the post-war generation's children are left with many more choices as they approach retirement.

Ready, Steady, Retire!: So what is the outlook for these Boomers in retirement?

Justin Urquhart Stewart: Whilst the Baby Boomer entering retirement having made sure he's got the right assets and pension provision is going to be relatively well-off, we know that life expectancy is set to continue increasing - and that is costly. We know a lot of these people are going to get ill in later life, and making sure pensions last to cover health and care costs may be a real challenge.

As for the next generation, quite frankly it's worrying. As their Boomer parents spend their hard-earned cash with enthusiasm, I fear for the next generation - the Busters are coming after the Boomers.

The outlook

The future patterns of work, health, care and income amongst Baby Boomers will be unique.

As they often have before, the post-war generation stand to redefine retirement, with the opportunity and facility to be explorative, enriching, and engaging. However, broad financial and social risks must be considered - both for individuals and for society as a whole.

The funding burden

The 22% increase in the 65-and-over population projected between 2012 and 2022 brings with it a number of challenges.

Projections are that the total number of older people using social care services, including residential and non-residential care, will increase - if they keep pace with demographic changes - from 2.0 million in 2010 to 3.2 million in 2030. That's an increase of around 60% over 20 years[17].

On a macroeconomic scale, changes in global economic patterns may make maintaining services and benefits for pensioners more challenging.

The likely cost to the NHS and public services more generally will be enormous. NESTA estimates that public spending on our ageing society could exceed £300 billion by 2025 as a result of the costs of social care, long-term health conditions, pensions and benefits[18]. British retirees are beginning to draw their pensions in growing numbers.

The growing cost of providing the state pension, alongside other aspects of state support (such as the NHS and social care) for those at the older end of the spectrum, makes it more important than ever that public policies targeted at this group are well designed, both for those who benefit from these policies and for those who pay for them.

Those who pay will have a stiff bill to foot. The social and economic tensions associated with funding future care for an ageing generation from a shrinking working age population are well documented.

In Britain, there are now more pensioners than there are children under 16. By 2025, more than half the population will be over 50.

As the number of people over 65 continues on trend to double in the next twenty years to over 16 million people - many of whom will require medical and social care - the impact on both our country's economy and society will be nothing short of unprecedented.

To put these figures into perspective we only need consider the dependency ratio, that is, the number of working adults financing each retired adult. This is shrinking, and shrinking rapidly, which puts the increasing burden of financing pensions and health care costs on fewer and fewer shoulders.

In 2014, there are four people of working age supporting each pensioner in Britain. By 2035, this number is expected to fall to 2.5, and to just two by 2050. That means a twofold increase in the cost-burden for each working person in Britain within one generation - 35 years[19].

Such predictions are supported by further research into the growing population of the very elderly. Between 2012 and 2035, the number of over-85s will double from 1.49 million to 3.48 million, equating to nearly 5% of the total UK population.

Similarly, the number of over-75s is projected to increase from 5.08 million to 8.92 million - equal to the entire population of Greater London. The Baby Boomers, only slightly younger than the individuals discussed here, continue to age, bringing their own social and economic pressures.

Providing at a local level

Predictable, growing demands for social care and health services mean that housing agencies and other local authority services are already beginning to experience the pressures of this ageing trend. The requirement for government at all levels to plan for the needs of ageing households in the future has never been greater to ensure a unified and broad-scale action plan is put in place to support Britain as its population ages.

Improved funding and scope for the Home Improvement Agency for example, which assists elderly residents in living comfortable, independent lives in their own homes, will help free nursing home places for the very ill.

Local council housing strategies must illustrate a desire to ensure that new housing is designed to meet the needs of older people. Such a considered approach will empower and enable the retirement community to move into more appropriate housing over time, lowering the cost of care and releasing under-occupied houses for families priced out of swelling markets.

Britain's long-term social planning remains insecure. As a result of generous social support programs, including pensions, over the last 50 years, government debts have continued to rise.

To tackle the issue, government has brought in changes and cuts to welfare programs and policies, including those directly affecting older people. The labour surge after the Second World War is unlikely to be replicated as a result of the projected demographic shifts, making a return to the expanding economy of the Boomer years very doubtful.

Expert view

We interviewed Donal Hegarty, Senior Manager for Commissioning for Adult Social Care for Surrey County Council, about the steps they are taking on a local level to address the growing ageing population.

Ready, Steady, Retire!: What sort of challenges do you foresee for County Councils like yours in Surrey as a result of the Baby Boomer generation retiring en masse over the next 20 years?

Donal Hegarty: The challenges are enormous, in the sense that we have an aging population which is increasingly going to put demands on services in an environment where the population of young people working is going to decrease as well. We're going to experience quite a large drain on public services. Because whilst as a nation people are living longer through improvements in technology, we also have to deal with the fact that people have more illnesses related to the aging process. If we take dementia as the example, dementia is one of the biggest challenges that faces not just this country, but the world.

Ready, Steady, Retire!: What steps do you think local authorities need to take to address these challenges?

Donal Hegarty: Public services are increasingly under the cosh financially and they have to look at how they work differently with people to provide the support they need. Councils should be thinking about how to work in a wider context by getting communities to be much more engaged with supporting people in their own local environment. This is quite a shift from the status quo, whereby people expect public services to deal with particular problems at any given point in time.

Our philosophy in Surrey is to support people to live at home, in the community, for as long as they choose to do so. If they choose to go into residential care we would support that also, but we want to make sure that we give people the opportunity to make the choice to stay and live in the environment where they have grown up and perhaps lived for 30 or 40 years.

Ready, Steady, Retire!: Do you have further examples of how local authorities are starting to respond to these challenges?

Donal Hegarty: In my experience, local authorities are really good at responding to these challenges. The biggest change is ensuring the various public services work together. It's an agenda that we call Public Transformation, whereby you get more integrated services between health and social care. Residents then receive a more integrated service between the police, the ambulance services and all public services working in a unified way.

I think the challenge for us - and I think it's one that we're actually embracing - is to take the next step and say that we can co-locate these services in a way that allows us to create pathways for people which are unified and seamless for them, whilst also being more efficient in terms of the costs involved and the logistics of providing these services.

Ready, Steady, Retire!: Can you talk to us more about what you are doing in Surrey specifically?

Donal Hegarty: As a County Council we, for instance, now co-locate with the 11 districts and boroughs that we work with. So we no longer have separate offices in the 11 districts and boroughs in Surrey. We're also engaged in projects looking at how we respond to call outs by the various emergency services in the most efficient and effective way.

Instead of having a call out for the ambulance service that is handled separately from a call out for the police, we're looking at how you might unify those in terms of effectiveness of response, but also better use of resources. That's the kind of thinking that's permeating through the way that we work presently.

We're also looking at unifying the workforce to work more efficiently and effectively, which means different ways of thinking. We're not stuck on procedure thinking, we want much more lateral thinking about how people can engage with communities.

Ready, Steady, Retire!: Can you give us an idea of the level of cost efficiencies you have achieved by implementing these initiatives in Surrey?

Donal Hegarty: The first thing to recognise is that we need to help people alter their expectations of the services that we, as a County Council, are able to provide. Historically, residents approached the Council with specific issues and expected services to be delivered to them. I don't think we can afford to do that anymore.

We have a program called 'Friends, Families & Communities' which is about saying that we want the community to be much more involved in determining their own help. So when someone comes to us the first thing we might ask is "What can you do for yourself?" or "What can your community do for you?"

In terms of specific efficiencies, we've been delivering cost savings in excess of £30 million for the last four or five years, just in adult social care, within Surrey County Council.

Ready, Steady, Retire!: That's very impressive. What do you think needs to be in place to achieve the level of results you are now experiencing?

Donal Hegarty: We are basically talking about needing to see cultural changes within the broader public services. In Surrey we have seen these changes happen quite quickly - more quickly with some services than with others. We're lucky enough to be part of what we call a Public Service Transformation Network.

We are actually at the forefront - Surrey is one of about nine local authorities in the country. We're working on specific projects that will enhance and accelerate that program of change because we are convinced that through better working together, we can deliver better services - alongside the much-needed efficiencies. The efficiencies are there to be made across all of the different agencies, which can only deliver value to our residents in other areas.

Inter-generational Conflict

For those looking towards retirement, financial tensions with the younger generation who will pay for university, struggle to get on the property ladder, and potentially accumulate heavy debt, may be inevitable.

Garry White, a commentator on equity markets, mentioned the same issue when interviewed by Ready, Steady, Retire!

He predicted an inter-generational conflict between young people and the Boomer generation, essentially because 'they've stolen all the wealth' - or so the argument goes. This pressure is weighing heavily on retirees' shoulders, as we explore in our chapter later on: the squeezed sandwich generation.

Government response

Economic worries will resonate with anyone planning for retirement. In a recent poll, more than a third of those nearing retirement singled out having enough money to live comfortably as the most important factor for them, only slightly behind health and well ahead of having a partner or rewarding family life[20].

Financial stresses and strains can add unwanted pressure to old age by restricting the travel plans and new activities that retirees may be hoping for.

Changes in government policy, intended to help address financial shortfalls in the short term will affect the financial realities of Baby Boomers. The Treasure is projecting that age related spending will increase from 20.4% of GDP in 2008 to 24.1% in 2020 and 26.1% by 2030[21].

In an effort to service those costs, retirement ages will rise gradually over the next few years, as funding for social programs and home care are both cut.

In the recent climate of financial austerity, very little attention has been paid to the direct effect this financial planning will have on older people. Building on Opportunity Age, the cross-government strategy on ageing from 2005, the Labour administration presented Building a Society for All Ages to Parliament in 2009, outlining plans to reform pensions, health and social care which have since been poorly implemented.

Investments in Partnerships for Older People projects (POPPs) and LinkAge Plus projects developed partnerships working in local areas and evaluations showed positive results for older people, though both have recently had their funding cut[22].

In 2010, David Cameron launched the Older People's Manifesto which claimed to place older people at the centre of politics. Considering this recent lip service, The Lords Select Committee on Public Service and Demographic Change recently concluded (2014) in a full financial review that the Cabinet had done little to initiate a long-term, coherent ageing strategy and accused the government of 'woeful unpreparedness'[23].

In conclusion

In a climate of continuing uncertainty and change, it is more important than ever that those approaching retirement take control of their future, identifying both their goals and aspirations and the financial measures necessary to enable those goals and guarantee their long-term security and comfort.

As this generation have sought to redefine every stage of adult life, they have been supported by a prospering economy, and evidence suggests those trends may not continue into the future. As long-term funding for social programs becomes increasingly unstable, retirees will have to harness the self-reliance and determination that has so characterised their generation to shape and secure their own future.

Although financial futures may be uncertain, this generation's retirements will be the first to be truly explored and enjoyed as a period of personal growth and exploration.

Fuelled by the longevity revolution and astonishing advances in health care, retirement will offer opportunities for personal fulfilment; learning new skills, exploring creative talents, and strengthening family relationships.

By planning for an independent and self-sufficient retirement, Baby Boomers can plan for a period when they can capitalise on these opportunities, creating an empowering retirement plan that will allow them to experience retirement as they have envisioned - secure, stimulating and full of joy.

Chapter Three
How to Retire Successfully

How to Retire Successfully

"It's not how old you are, it's how you are old." - Jules Renard

Liberated by their wealth, more active lifestyles and new technology, the post-war generation is challenging traditional attitudes towards retirement.

Today's new retirees are not happy with the staid, conservative model of retirement as it was known to their parents. Instead, this generation is seeking out a new sense of freedom and empowerment. Their goals and aspirations have become an essential part of the retirement planning process.

As they approach retirement, many members of the post-war generation are seriously examining how they can live their lives to feel fulfilled.

Fear that retirement will bring an activity void is common, as are concerns that, in retirement, life may lack a sense of individual purpose. For many people approaching retirement, a sedate, self-destructive boredom is what they fear most deeply.

At the point of retiring 1 in 5 of the retirees we surveyed were concerned about how they would fill their time[24]. This needn't be the case.

A well-planned retirement should offer the time, opportunity, and freedom to pursue individual goals and interests. Retirement is an opportunity for you to call the shots, run at your own pace - which is often the first opportunity many people have to live their lives this way.

For many, the unknowns of retirement are a frightening prospect. Alongside financial concerns some Boomers struggle with complex philosophical issues; purpose, self-belief, and the frightening prospect of perhaps no longer being in complete control of their personal situation.

It is impossible to ignore that retirement is a challenging period of adjustment; in the US 41% say retirement was the hardest adjustment of their lives[25]. But it is important to remember that it is simply an adjustment.

The post-war generation has successfully fought to redefine age and ageing in the UK at every stage of life, and there is no reason why that vitality and spirit should collapse at retirement.

Every single one of the challenges mentioned here can be addressed and planned for. Admittedly not all challenges can be averted, but being aware of what may be waiting for you around the corner must be beneficial.

Retirement offers an extraordinary opportunity for growth and development. Almost two thirds of the retirees we spoke to were looking forward to all the things they could do, now they had the time. Creating a holistic vision for retirement at every stage opens up many exciting opportunities.

Planning across the phases

Retirement is often misunderstood as a fundamentally financial and economic event. Instead, it represents a thorough transformation of adult life. Baby Boomers, with their unparalleled good health, financial security, and opportunities for growth and expansion in old age have redefined ageing, but sometimes fail to appreciate that their newly redefined retirement will require a well-considered plan.

Viewed as a whole life event, successful retirement planning demands a holistic approach that integrates aspirations, needs and responsibilities with the more traditional material goals. Our definition of a satisfying retirement is this:

You can do what you want to do.

Retirement is no longer one distinct phase of life. Instead it can, broadly speaking, be broken down into three separate phases - each with very different consequences for work and life in general.

"Pre-retirement" or "entering retirement" generally refers to those entering and adjusting to retirement. The true "vital retirement years" refers to those aged between 65 and roughly 74 - or later for some - who have retired fully and are enjoying the fruits of their labour, whilst the "long-term" retired or "period of later life" refer to those in the latter stage of retirement, normally over 75.

Many people retiring now and those looking eagerly forward to their retirement see their sixties and early 70s as decades of opportunity. Free of work, without a financially dependent family and still in good health, many Baby

Boomers view these years as the time to enjoy activities that they didn't have the time for during their working years.

For the peace of mind necessary to enjoy and capitalise on this opportunity, it's important to consider how to fund all phases of retirement as it is now defined.

The key to successful retirement planning is making sure you are asking yourself the right questions. In our experience, the most pressing concerns of those approaching retirement are related to how and when they should take their pensions benefits, as opposed to the more profound and challenging questions like "What's important to me to feel fulfilled in my retirement?"

A qualified Financial Planner with experience of working with those planning their retirement can help ask the right questions at the right time. Answering challenging questions about the things most important to you will give you the best chance of achieving the life in retirement you most desire.

Whilst consideration of how to fund an increasingly longer retirement is crucial, without a proper understanding of what would make a successful retirement for you, the money can become meaningless.

Funding retirement

Whilst longevity is a blessing, it does require consideration, especially where money is concerned. With the Baby Boomer generation set to live on average 34 years longer than their grandparents[26], the pressure on funding these additional years can be huge.

This generation is renowned for being a generation of savers, at times astonished at the carefree attitudes of their children or grandchildren with regards to money. Brought up with the belief that you saved before spending - and fortunate enough to benefit from healthy final salary pensions - many Boomers are entering retirement in a relatively healthy financial position.

While no generation is homogenous, and poverty is an issue for some Baby Boomers, many are better off than those who retired before them. According to the ONS, the average gross income for pensioners increased by about 50% in real terms between 1994-95 and 2010-11[27]. Ensuring pension pots last for such a length of time, however, remains a concern for many.

Only 7% of adults in their 50s have no financial worries about their retirement. Concerns about returns on savings (23%) and the stability of investments (11%) demonstrate the anxiety many people feel going into retirement[28]. By planning for both the material and emotional aspects of each of these phases, retirees have a better chance of finding the confidence and security that is essential to taking the best advantage of retirement as a period of personal growth.

Case Study - Funding retirement

Dr. Gerard Clelland, alongside his recently-retired wife Susie, looked toward his own retirement from a successful GP practice with some trepidation.

He wanted to make sure that his investments were sound and to understand what he should do with the additional £200,000 he would be receiving as a lump sum from his pension scheme on retirement.

The couple came to see us and we illustrated that they were asking the wrong questions. Instead of asking how they should invest Gerard's lump sum, they should have been asking 'Have we got enough income to meet our expenditure requirements in retirement?' Both Gerard and Susie were looking forward to opportunities to travel in their retirement.

Gerard and Susie's lifetime cash flow forecast illustrated that they didn't need to invest the money, as they had enough income to meet their requirements for their lifetimes as a result of healthy final salary pensions.

Instead, we advised they could spend the lump sum and enjoy the early years of their retirement whilst they still had the vitality to do so. Gerard and Susie felt an enormous sense of relief and freedom to be able to enter retirement safe in the knowledge they could afford to live the life that would make them fulfilled.

Expert view

We spoke to Fiona Tait, president of The Insurance Society of Edinburgh and a leading technical pensions expert, about the need to plan for all stages of retirement.

Ready, Steady, Retire!: What issues will Baby Boomers specifically face in retirement?

Fiona Tait: The traditional image of retirees has changed dramatically over the last few years. As pension companies we have changed our marketing material quite a lot. The traditional image of somebody in slippers is no longer relevant. Today's retiree seems younger, fitter and much more active.

The main issue financially is that they will probably spend more money in their retirement. Their more active lifestyles require funding. Today's retirees have worked hard all their lives and they think that now is the time to enjoy it on a beautiful holiday, or to support a new hobby. These types of activities result in higher levels of spending than if they were more traditionally, perhaps, sitting at home.

Ready, Steady, Retire!: Will the longevity of Boomers make all that saving harder?

Fiona Tait: The leading edge of the Boomers are more likely to be in final salary arrangements, which takes away a lot of the concerns about funding their retirement, and even the decisions they need to make. Their pensions will seamlessly turn into an income stream when they retire, which makes life quite easy.

We've got another ten to 15 years of this wave to go through before we reach the later tranche of Baby Boomers, who will possibly have slightly different problems. Because they're more likely to be in a defined contribution pension arrangement, where an awful lot more choices have to be made by the individual, they really do need to make sure they've saved enough.

Ready, Steady, Retire!: What's the most difficult part of planning for an increasingly long retirement?

Fiona Tait: I think the most difficult part honestly is that we just don't manage the perception and reality gap well at all. You want people to enjoy the younger years, whilst also planning for the more expensive later ones.

I believe the idea that a life of leisure is what today's retirees are looking for, either financially or personally, is just unrealistic. But we need to help people to plan effectively so that they can make the most of their early retirement years whilst they have the vitality and vigour to do so, whilst still being able to fund their more expensive later life.

The role of work

For many, leaving work represents a seismic shift. For decades, a life of ease has been marketed as the ultimate retirement goal. The reality for many is that without the contrast of meaningful labour - whether paid or unpaid - leisure loses its meaning.

A career is often a key component of how people define themselves and recent retirees must grapple with what giving up work means for both their own identities and their priorities in later life. Adopting a phased approach to retirement can smooth this transition, allowing for a greater degree of financial freedom, as well as personal fulfilment.

Historically, leaving work has been seen as a source of freedom - a boon of leisure time that can be used as productively or unproductively as you choose.

In fact, early retirement has been heralded as the ultimate goal for many hardworking executives and blue-collar workers alike. As Boomers retire, many are redefining this phase of life by continuing to pursue the careers and goals that were important to them, or using the time to explore new commercial ventures and ideas.

The growing number of retirees returning to work helps to illustrate the importance and relevance of work for many; in the US, over one in three of all retirees return to work in some guise within one year of retiring. The same trends are true in the UK; the employment rate for people aged 65 and over has increased steadily in the past decade from 5% in 2001 to 9% in 2012[29].

The longevity of the post-war generation will challenge many assumptions about older people in the workforce.

As the state pension age rises, both men and women will remain in paid work for longer. Increasingly, employers support and understand this development in working patterns, especially among those in their late fifties or early sixties who are still very integrated with their work communities.

More mature employees often hold a bank of experience and knowledge that is still valuable in their retirement years and could perhaps be contributed either through a part-time or consultancy position, or increasingly by continuing in a full-time job.

Flexible and varied patterns of work are becoming the norm for older employees. In 2012, 29% of 50-64 year-olds in the UK, and 67% of those over 65, worked part time[30].

As many Baby Boomers leave with generous pensions and reward schemes as a result of history's greatest bull market, companies will need to start competing with the lure of retirement by offering a huge variety of non-financial benefits to retirees; flexibility, a sense of belonging in the workplace, a sense of personal satisfaction from what they accomplish - all things that bring a sense of purpose and boost self-esteem.

Gradual increases in the state pension age are particularly important for women. Women's state pension age is predicted to rise more quickly than men's, and they are the demographic for which long-term health is most likely to improve, adding important productive working years to their lives.

16% of 65- to 69-year-old women were in work in 2010–11 and we expect this to rise to 37% within a decade. Employment rates for women in their late 60s, which are already at their highest level since the late 1960s, are set to increase faster, approaching or even overtaking men in the early 2020s[31].

For women in this generation, this represents the culmination of years of hard work establishing meaningful and satisfying careers and offering a chance to continue into the future. Women who may have been daunted at the thought of losing an important part of their identity have the opportunity to continue to define themselves in a multi-faceted way in retirement.

The increases in projected employment rates of older women mean we can estimate that, by 2018–19, 60- to 64-year-old women will be as likely to be in paid work as 60- to 64-year-old men, with the equivalent being true of 65- to 69-year-olds by 2020–21[32].

For a generation of women who fought for equality, the opportunity to maintain their working identities in retirement should be considered a deeply important one.

Maintaining a sense of satisfaction by continuing to be productive - either through work or some other route - is an important component of retirement planning for both men and women. New scientific and sociological research suggests that working beyond the traditional retirement age has positive benefits for all, helping keep the older generation - particularly those without close families or communities - involved, vital, and physically and mentally much healthier.

For many, working provides a sense of mattering and being connected with other people. Staying involved in work in some capacity also has benefits for those wishing to keep mentally sharp and focused.

For many, to deny the importance of work in some capacity, whether it be continuing a profession past the usual retirement age or even starting a new business, is an important and meaningful aspect of life. It is certainly one that should be considered a feasible component of most people's retirement.

Case Study - Creating a meaningful retirement

Clive Holiday was 61 and on the board of a major retail company when he made the decision to retire. Increasingly dissatisfied with the way the business was being run, Clive made the decision to resign, and found himself retired, rather unexpectedly.

Whilst his financial future was secure as a result of a healthy final salary pension, Clive was unprepared for how he would live in retirement to feel fulfilled and to fill his days in a meaningful way.

Clive often found himself getting into his car each morning and heading out as though he were driving to work, but instead he drove to the newsagent or local shop.

Within a couple of months Clive was approached by business contacts at smaller retailers who asked whether he would consider becoming a non-executive director. Whilst this was not a move that Clive had planned, these positions provided him with a sense of purpose in his retirement.

In parallel, Clive became both a governor of his old preparatory school and heavily involved with advising his city's Symphony Orchestra on business strategy and marketing - on a voluntary basis.

By establishing a pattern of part-time and volunteer work, Clive was able to retain the sense of purpose he took pride in during his working days and marry it with a rewarding sense of community involvement and a more relaxed working schedule.

By taking advantage of opportunities that arose and seeking out new meaningful work, Clive was able to formulate a retirement that worked for him.

Retirement by choice

Some people may not want to retire when they reach the traditional retirement age, but they do want to know that they could retire if they chose to. Sadly, a return to work in retirement is occasionally dictated by financial necessity.

Private pension arrangements are often an important factor in whether men remain in full-time work.

In a recent study, men with defined benefit pension schemes were far less likely to return to work than those with less generous retirement schemes, and men with outstanding debts or mortgages were far more likely to remain in full-time work than those without. There are many reasons why you may decide to remain in employment beyond the traditional retirement date; financial necessity is certainly the least desirable.

Creating a plan for your retirement can help alleviate concerns about funding all stages of retirement and allow you to focus on maintaining a sense of productivity and purpose in ways which uniquely benefit you.

Making a difference

A life of ease is very rarely one's true retirement goal. Many retirees have found days of golf and fishing are not nearly as interesting as they were led to believe, and abruptly ending work can bring its own challenges; without the contrast and paradox of meaningful labour, leisure often loses its meaning and boredom can soon set in.

Thankfully, a well-planned retirement can bring unique options for empowerment and self-fulfilment.

As a time of transition, retirement offers an opportunity to redress life's imbalances. The hours of long commutes, working away from home and lack of time with the family or enjoying leisure activities can finally be compensated for. For many Boomers, retirement is a time to rebuild personal connections, becoming more involved in family life as they support their children and grandchildren.

Others work with charities or religious groups to help support broader communities; such opportunities offer a unique chance to reinvest in the communities with which Boomers have long-standing connections.

We see new retirees passionately involved in their old schools and colleges, helping transfer a lifetime of knowledge to the next generation, or spearheading campaigns among neighbourhoods and local communities to improve conditions for everyone.

Communities prosper enormously from the impact of knowledgeable residents volunteering and engaging with community organisations, so a commitment to volunteering in retirement brings benefits to retirees and communities alike.

Many non-profit organisations are seeing a huge growth in the number of retirees involved in volunteer work. Over 20% of those aged 60-69 volunteer at least once a month, a marked increase from around 15% for those in their fifties. According to a study in the United States, the number of volunteers over age 65 could grow by 50% during the next decade[33].

Expert view

We interviewed Ray Nottage, head of Christchurch Borough Council in Dorset about the impact the retired population of Christchurch has upon the local community.

Ready, Steady, Retire!: I understand that one in three of Christchurch's residents is retired. How would you describe the town?

Cllr Nottage: Christchurch is the retirement capital of the UK but it doesn't feel like that. It's not a sedentary community. It's a very active community, irrespective of age. As far as the grey pound is concerned, it's a very stable influence on our overall economy.

Ready, Steady, Retire!: How does the community benefit from having such a high proportion of retirees?

Cllr Nottage: One of the things that we have been consciously doing is creating more community activities for our residents. Recognising the fact many retirees wish to remain actively involved with their community and in some form of rewarding work, we have created partnerships that allow volunteers to run some of our community centres and such like.

For example, all of our tourist information centres are now run by volunteers - the majority of whom are retired and looking for a meaningful, worthwhile cause to support. This has been a hugely successful venture as the retired population gets actively involved in the social aspects of our community.

Christchurch is a very involved community, which brings commercial benefits with it. We would not be able to keep some of our facilities operating without the voluntary support of our retired community.

Ready, Steady, Retire!: What do you see retirees of Christchurch getting up to?

Cllr Nottage: I myself am retired but have been working incredibly hard as Head of Christchurch Borough Council for the past six years and I see a lot of other people doing the same thing. It's amazing really what some of these guys get up to. I see them windsurfing, boating and surfing.

The other day I saw a group of retired men starting a game of 'walking football' - just like regular football, but you walk around the pitch instead of running. The first guy came out and he was 79. There he was in his shorts and old football boots and he said, "I love this. It's unbelievable."

Ready, Steady, Retire!: What could other areas learn from Christchurch, as the retirement capital of the UK?

Cllr Nottage: I think the conditions that we have created in the town present a very interesting perspective for other areas in how to deal with an ageing population. We're the retirement capital of the country because there's so much going on and we've created a very involved community.

Achieving Fulfilment

The time offered by retirement is a catalyst; it is the missing ingredient, for many, that prevented them from pursuing the interests and skills that they feel complete them. Retirement offers a time to pursue creative passions and intellectual interests.

Language classes and art studio time are freely available to retirees, whilst others turn to meditation or spiritual practice to help further a sense of self. Each year, hundreds of retirees launch new businesses and ventures in retirement.

Travel often plays an important part of many retirement plans. Whether local or exotic, retirement offers the time, flexibility and freedom to travel extensively, or perhaps even move to a dreamt-of seaside cottage or country house to allow a full sense of connection with a world that often flew by through train windows on a morning commute.

When viewed as a complete, holistic and transitional experience, retirement is - as an opportunity - truly unparalleled.

Later life

Generally speaking, Baby Boomers are probably the most fortunate retiring generation in history.

As previously mentioned, the average gross income for pensioners has increased by about 50% in real terms between 1994-95 and 2010-11, meaning that many people retiring today are likely to be financially comfortable in their later years. Even given this security, Baby Boomers face a number of important decisions as they look towards later retirement.

In later life, emotive and personal issues can become entangled in financial ones, and sensitive Financial Planning should consider both aspects. Downsizing is a consideration for many in later life and illustrates these complexities.

Having spent over fifty years in their family home, a retired couple with countless memories and personal attachments will understandably be intensely anxious about the prospect of leaving. Where would they go? They may well not be able to establish the same community links in a new town, depriving them of practical or emotional support.

If staying in, and maintaining, the family home is financially plausible, is staying put the right decision?

It can be difficult, on many levels, to face the prospect of clearing out years of memories and all your belongings and trying to squeeze them into a much smaller place. The prospect of downsizing is always difficult, and is one that many retirees don't seriously consider until later life, when the practicalities of managing their home become unfeasible.

Financial considerations, including mortgages and upkeep costs should be closely considered alongside emotional ones.

Passing on wealth

As the post-war generation ages, thoughts turn to how best to pass on their wealth to their loved ones.

As the parents of Baby Boomers pass away, many find themselves inheriting money, which can complicate their own estate planning further. As we have already revealed, more than 80% of the nation's £6.7 trillion wealth is owned by Baby Boomers.

Of the £2.6 trillion in shares or savings, Boomers own more than £1 trillion, as well as 40% of the £2.5 trillion tied up in property. Boomers account for a third of Britain's £1.8 trillion in pensions. Having a home has proved such an astonishingly good investment that 1 in 5 Boomers owns a second home[34].

It's no wonder then that many Baby Boomers enter retirement with estates worth in excess of the nil rate band applicable for Inheritance Tax (IHT).

When inheriting from their parents, this windfall can increase their estate's IHT liability yet further, so seeking specific tax advice from a qualified wealth manager is advisable at this stage to ensure wealth inherited by Baby Boomers is done so as tax efficiently as possible. In some cases it is sensible to bypass the Boomers and pass the money straight on to the next generation.

This has the effect of not increasing the value of the Boomers' estates, while perhaps providing their children with a step onto the property ladder, at a time when the average age of first time buyers is higher than ever before.

As Boomers then look to passing their wealth on to their own children, a fully informed consideration of their financial needs throughout retirement is essential to long-term financial security. This means considering what the retirees' expenditure needs will be for the rest of their lives, taking account of possible care home funding, to ensure that wealth isn't passed on too early.

Planning when is the best time to transfer wealth to children and grandchildren can be difficult. With their children's best interests at heart, many retirees have mixed feelings on when wealth is most efficiently transferred to the next generation.

The phenomenon of "shirtsleeves to shirtsleeves in three generations" is a well-documented one; one generation starts with nothing but through a process of hard-work manages to amass and build up wealth, saving carefully for the long-term benefit of their family. The next generation inherits their parents' hard work ethos and manages to continue to build the family's wealth, only to see those precious savings squandered by their children through poor investment choices or unwise spending habits.

Unfortunately the values of hard-work and saving have not been adopted by the third generation, as they have never had to work for anything themselves.

Speaking about money frankly within families is often difficult. If discussions about how and when wealth should be transferred are left until the later stages of retirement, this can become a highly emotional and incredibly challenging discussion, for everyone involved.

To ensure that your family can use inherited wealth to their best advantage it is wise to talk about your wishes as early as possible.

How to pass on wealth

The process of transferring wealth can be accomplished either through pure gifts or by setting up trusts. Whilst gifts offer freedom from any further financial planning, they also offer no control over the use of the assets transferred.

Trusts, in which designated administrators are given responsibility for holding and distributing assets according to terms laid out in a trust document, offer a more controlled solution. Money, property, land, buildings and investments can all be distributed through trusts, held safe until they are given to the legal beneficiaries according to your wishes as the trust's settlor, or creator.

Key reasons to establish a trust

1. To ensure better control and protection over family assets.

2. To allow you choice in when the beneficiaries receive a benefit.

3. To save inheritance tax.

4. To pass money or property over to specific people when you die – known as a will Trust

5. Gifts to children for house purchase can provide protection in case of divorce or bankruptcy.

6. For intergenerational wealth transfer benefits. You can provide for the grandchildren as well as the children.

When planning to transfer your wealth, it is important to remember that Inheritance Tax is almost certainly a consideration. No longer simply a tax for the very wealthy, many Baby Boomers find themselves paying Inheritance Tax based on the sheer value of their homes, without taking account of additional investments and savings.

- There are several strategies that may help reduce your inheritance tax liability.

- Gifts given whilst you are alive and up to seven years before your death will be tax free, making some gift-giving a possibly valuable option to explore in wealth transfer.

- Smaller gifts may be Inheritance Tax free depending on current IHT exemption levels.

- Gifts to charities are also Inheritance Tax free, and leaving 10% of your income or more will reduce your Inheritance Tax liability from 40 to 36%.

- Due to the variations of family trusts and regular changes in taxation it is advisable to seek the advice of a specialist trust advisor and tax expert who can advise on specific circumstances including any tax implications.

Make a will

Advancing age will also necessitate a frank discussion about death and dying. Understandably, for many, this is the single most unpleasant prospect of financial planning in later life. 61% of UK adults do not have a will, with the most commonly given reason being that they just "haven't gotten around to it". Perhaps more likely is a deep determination to avoid the issue altogether.

More worryingly, "not getting round to it" is an increasingly common excuse as we age. More than half of 55-65 year-olds have still "not gotten around to it"[35].

Without confronting this uncomfortable topic, the distribution of your assets will be at the mercy of a maze of intestacy rules and regulations. For Baby Boomers who have accumulated substantial wealth and assets over the course of their lifetime, drafting a will is particularly important if you hope to provide for partners, loved ones, friends and family.

Under current intestacy rules, in the case of no children, all of a deceased's assets will go directly to their spouse or civil partner, whilst if children are present, the deceased's assets will be split between their spouse and children.

Whilst this may sound like a reasonable division of assets, without drafting a will you have no chance to appoint an executor of your estate or make known beneficiaries outside of your immediate family. Considering how you would like your assets distributed after your death is an essential part of comprehensive retirement and wealth transfer planning.

Case Study - Planning for after you're gone

Michael and Julia Barton were both in their 70s and very much settled in to their retirement when they began seriously worrying about not having planned sufficiently for Julia's financial security, in the event that Michael predeceased her.

They had both remarried and on doing so, Julia had lost her entitlement to her deceased first husband's army widow's pension. This was of particular concern as there was a limited spouse's pension payable from Michael's pension on his death.

The couple had relatives living in Australia who they wanted to visit, but they were concerned whether they could afford to, and so were saving hard out of pension income to achieve this dream. The fear of eating in to savings and investments destined to support Julia in the event of Michael's death was paramount.

They came to us for advice and we created their Financial Plan. They were immediately reassured so see that their lifetime cash flow forecast illustrated they could afford to visit their relatives now. Importantly, they would still have enough funds to support their later years.

Sadly Michael died this year, after successfully visiting Australia a couple of years previously, and Julia's war widow's pension has been successfully reinstated, with our help. The whole exercise for Michael and Julia allowed them to travel, safe in the knowledge they were both financially secure for their future.

Steps you can take for a successful retirement

There's no need to be fearful of retirement. Retirement is no longer the final act. And it need not represent either an insurmountable financial burden or a fundamental change to the values and principles that are important to you.

Instead retirement is an extraordinary opportunity to re-evaluate and redefine personal goals, with extra resources of time, money and perspective available.

Here are some suggestions for achieving a successful retirement:

Talk it over. Having frank conversations with your family, friends and - if you choose - a Financial Planner offer an opportunity to consider and refine what it is you will need to be fulfilled in retirement. Clear goals and honest discussions help foster a sense of purpose and achievement that has been proven to be a key driver of happiness in retirement.

Create a plan. By considering all aspects of retirement, rather than purely the financial, you can explore whether or not your finances will support your chosen lifestyle, and consider the provisions you need to make to ensure your comfort and security throughout your retirement. However unpleasant it may be, retirement's later stages must be considered too - don't be afraid to plan for care costs.

Decide about the role of work. Remember that your retirement will most probably last a long time, and that all phases must be considered and discussed. In early retirement, take time to reconsider your work, whether your preferred path be to remain working, shift to different responsibilities, or perhaps start a new business altogether.

Get out there. If volunteer work is a more engaging option, explore it, alongside life goals like travel and developing family relationships to ensure you get the most out of your retirement years.

Pass it on. Discuss whom you would like to pass your estate on to, as well as exploring with a tax advisor how to transfer your wealth and assets effectively and efficiently.

Above all, remember that this is a plan for your benefit and empowerment. Review your goals and aspirations regularly, as well as the security you are receiving from your financial arrangements.

It's reasonable to expect that priorities may change, surprises may happen, and goals may be redefined. By approaching retirement with a clear, open, and focused mind, your later years can be an astonishing time of personal opportunity and growth.

Life at any age can be challenging. In retirement, those challenges can be met with energy, resources, and a lifetime of experience. Combined with clear advice and thorough planning, you will be in the best possible position to make decisions for yourself and your future.

Chapter Four
Rise of the Silver Splitter

Rise of the Silver Splitter

"My husband and I have never considered divorce...murder sometimes, but never divorce." - Joyce Brothers

As Baby Boomers retire, they are bucking national trends and divorcing in growing numbers. Over the past twenty years alone, the number of over 60s getting divorced has risen by nearly 75%[36].

Good quality relationships are critical for wellbeing in retirement. Baby Boomers need to understand this silver splitter phenomenon and the steps they can take to enhance healthy relationships throughout retirement.

A recent poll for the counselling service Relate found that 83% of older people agreed having strong personal relationships with friends and family was the single most important factor for a happy retirement[37].

If you are planning for a happy retirement, the quality of your relationships counts. This includes the relationship you have with your significant other.

One large-scale study in the US back in the 1970s found that satisfaction with marriage and family life was the most accurate predictor of overall life satisfaction. If you're unhappy with your personal relationships, chances are you are going to be unhappy in life generally.

Other research has discovered a correlation between subjective well-being and the number of relationships which are maintained in retirement. People generally do a good job of maintaining relationships when they first retire, but these relationships can trail off during their seventies and eighties, resulting in a noticeable decline in reported well-being.

The challenge

The most recent year for official divorce figures is 2011. During this year, 15,300 men or women over 60 in the UK were granted a divorce. This compares with just 8,700 20 years earlier in 1991[38].

Divorce rates for the over 60s are rising sharply while fewer under 60s are getting divorced than ever before, after the divorce rate peaked in the early 1990s.

What is driving this 'silver splitter' phenomenon and why is it so important for Baby Boomers to understand as a part of their retirement planning?

According to the Office for National Statistics (ONS), the dramatic improvement in life expectancy is one factor influencing a rising divorce rate among retired couples. In fact, the ONS pointed to rising life expectancy as the main driver behind the rise of the silver splitter.

Cultural attitudes could also be playing a role. A more relaxed attitude towards separation and divorce is adopted by the post-war generation than was demonstrated by their parents or grandparents. Marriage is no longer for life, with 34% of marriages in the UK ending in divorce before the 20th wedding anniversary, according to the ONS.

Only 16% of marriages make it until the 60th wedding anniversary[39], although the death of a spouse remains the main reason for this statistic, rather than divorce. On average, a marriage in the UK is currently lasting for 32 years, which many would consider a reasonably good achievement.

Another driver behind the rise in silver splitters is growing financial independence for women. No longer is it the case that men control the purse strings in a typical household. Shared responsibility for household earnings and expenditure creates more freedom for women to make choices about divorce, safe in the knowledge that the courts usually award a fair and equitable settlement.

For over a decade now, courts have used the starting point of an equal split of assets when deciding on a financial settlement. It's also possible to split and equalise pension assets, which provides women, most often, with a good sense of financial security in retirement.

The disproportionate amount of wealth owned by the Baby Boomers means they can often afford to divorce, spreading joint financial resources across two lives and maintaining desirable lifestyles; something the younger generations struggle to achieve when they are burdened with debt. Divorce is a less attractive prospect when you will be awarded half a mortgage rather than half a house.

The latest ONS figures also found that men over 60 are as likely as women over 60 to file for divorce. This is in contrast to the overall population where women are far more likely to petition their husband for divorce than vice versa. For the entire adult population, two-thirds of divorces are initiated by women.

It could be the result of a delayed midlife crisis, or possibly men waiting until responsibilities to their families had been fulfilled, once children had left home, before finishing an unhappy relationship.

Celebrity role models probably don't help. In recent years we have seen a publicly acrimonious split between 70 year old John Cleese and his 64 year old (third) wife, Faye Eichelberger, following 16 years of marriage[40].

Iconic Baby Boomer and 60-something rock star Ronnie Wood recently divorced his wife of 23 years, trading her in for a much younger model.

Bill Nighy and Diana Quick, both in their 60s, called time on their marriage after 27 years together. Most Boomers will of course not be influenced by these celebrity separations, but they do illustrate a growing trend.

Absent carers

Another consequence of divorce in retirement is the absence of a potential carer in later life. A politician recently suggested that silver splitters are placing growing pressure on the adult social care system, because more people are living alone when the need for long-term care arises.

He went as far as suggesting that family doctors should talk to their older patients about the health of their relationships, directing them to counselling services where appropriate in an effort to stem the rising number of silver split-ters and reduce pressure on care services.

Writing for a national newspaper in March 2014, senior Conservative MP Andrew Selous recounted the following tale:

"A friend recently told me that between them his parents had one set of eyes that worked, one set of ears and one set of legs. They lived together with minimal support. Had they split up the care costs for both of them would have been significant."

Staying together simply to minimise the cost to the state of providing your care in later life doesn't sound like a good enough reason to drag out a terminally unhappy relationship. This does, however, illustrate a potential consequence of crowds of Baby Boomers heading to the family courts to get their decree absolute.

Rising life expectancy could also be placing growing pressure on relationships in retirement.

Living for longer means that one partner in a relationship is more likely to experience serious health conditions, resulting in the need for care. Existing cracks in relationships can be stressed as a spouse or partner is forced to take on the role of carer for loved ones, dramatically changing the dynamic of a relationship.

Moving into residential care is another factor which can strain even the strongest relationships in retirement. What is effectively a forced separation, often for the first time in a lifetime together, can become intolerable, resulting in big changes to daily activities or even geographic location.

Dangers of divorce

Living as a couple is good for us, according to most measures. Life expectancy for a single person in retirement is anywhere from four to seven years shorter than for a couple.

According to life expectancy tables in the US, 65 year olds might expect to live until they are 85 or 82, for a single woman and single man respectively. This is anywhere from 15-30% shorter than for a married couple at age 65, who have a joint life expectancy of 89 years[41].

This isn't all bad news, of course. A shorter life expectancy means spending plans in retirement can be adjusted, with the aim of spending more during a shorter period of time in order to realise all of your goals during your lifetime.

Being married also has consequences for health. Married couples experience lower morbidity rates than single people, with a lower risk of heart attacks, cancer and requiring a major surgery[42]. The quality of the marriage is as important here as the act of being married, but in general terms those with stronger relationships have a 50% reduced risk of 'all-cause mortality'.

It's been argued that married couples being generally healthier than single people is the result of both selection and protection effects. This means that healthy people are more likely to get married than unhealthy people. Once married, the relationship brings a combination of resources and social support.

Loneliness

Concerns are also being raised about loneliness. The charity Relate has warned about the dangers stemming from Baby Boomers living alone in retirement. This is due to become the norm rather than the exception, as the divorce rate for the over 60s continues to rise.

When the kids leave home and relationships fail, loneliness is often the end result.

Research published by the Office for National Statistics found that nearly seven million Baby Boomers in the UK admit to feeling lonely. This rises to nearly half of all over 80 year olds, as the older generations more acutely feel the weight of loneliness than younger retirees who perhaps have more social opportunities available to explore.

According to the Campaign to End Loneliness, 10% of people over the age of 65 in the UK, which equates to nearly one million people, are lonely all or most of the time. Those who report this level of loneliness believe it has a negative impact on their physical and mental health, and overall quality of life. This is a shocking statistic and Baby Boomers need to take active steps to avoid loneliness in retirement.

Being widowed tends to trump divorce as a catalyst for loneliness in retirement, but both are key drivers of a sense of isolation in later life. The research suggests that women feel loneliness more acutely than men, probably due to their increased longevity resulting in a greater number surviving a spouse.

And loneliness can be a real killer, with one US study finding a 14% increased risk of death among people who consistently feel lonely in retirement[43].

Despite the prevalence of loneliness in the retired population, and its dire implications, Baby Boomers don't always view it as a major concern. This might be because many Baby Boomers refuse to view themselves as old or indeed ageing, instead taking the view they are only as old as they feel.

With Baby Boomers entering retirement in ever growing numbers, they will be on the front-line of a loneliness epidemic. It's currently forecast that the number of people over age 65 living alone is set to rise from 3 million to 4.8 million by 2033. That represents a 60% increase in single living in retirement within the next 20 years.

Five ways to tackle loneliness in retirement

Everyone is different, so making a conscious effort to increase levels of social engagement in retirement is not a blanket solution. Addressing loneliness in later life does require an action plan however.

Here are a few suggestions for getting out there in retirement, making new friends and generally combating loneliness.

Get an education. Life-long learning is a great way to find like-minded peers who share similar interests. The University of the Third Age (U3A) is run by its members with local groups in most towns and villages across the UK. Find your local group and learn about their courses at www.u3a.org.uk.

Become a volunteer. Volunteering is a great way to combat loneliness, making new friends and devoting energy to something productive. Find volunteering opportunities in your area with Volunteering England at www.volunteering.org.uk.

Become a silver surfer. A think-tank recently suggested that retirees should receive training to use the Internet as a way to tackle the growing loneliness epidemic. As things stand, four in ten over-65s do not use the Internet at home and more than five million retired people in the UK have never been online. Email, Skype and social networking are all ways of dealing with social isolation, according to the Policy Exchange think-tank.

Get an allotment. For those who enjoy the outside life, getting an allotment is a great form of exercise and a way to address social isolation. Many retirees use it as an excuse to get out of the house, interact with others and hone their green-fingered gardening skills. With many allotments having committees to keep them in good running order, opportunities for socialisation are plenty.

Join a community group. If you want to give something back to local society, there are a great many community groups looking for new members that are often better at addressing local needs than national or even regional charities. Depending on your interests and experience, you might join a community group covering community-service and action, health, educational, personal growth and improvement, social welfare and self-help for the disadvantaged.

Friends as well as lovers

The importance of quality relationships in retirement extends beyond those you maintain with your spouse or partner.

The Mental Health Foundation recently found that 74% of the Baby Boomer generation have friends and family who they felt would provide valuable support in the future. Without this support, you could be left without an important support network in retirement.

Strong support networks, which include friends and family, have repeatedly been shown to offer protection against illness, allowing retirees to live longer, healthier, happier lives. Those who are active in their communities in retirement are more likely to maintain better mental health than their less active peers.

Case Study – The financial implications of living alone

As a divorcee entering retirement at a relatively young 61 years old, Sally had amassed a small amount of savings as a result of the financial settlement following her divorce some years earlier. But as a part-time teacher in receipt of a pension from part-time earnings - being solely responsible for raising her sons she hadn't been able to work full-time - she was not particularly well off.

Sally's major concern was being able to fund her modest lifestyle in retirement. She had two sons, one of whom lived in Canada, and it was important to Sally that she could afford to visit her son every year.

Sally had kept the family home to raise her sons, but was not keen to downsize at this stage of her life, although she agreed she would probably do so in her later years. She was looking for advice on choosing the most appropriate investments as Sally felt she hadn't made the best choices over the years.

Even though she lived fairly frugally, as a single person Sally's outgoings were disproportionately higher than most individuals living as a couple. She was very concerned about making ends meet.

Sally sought advice and her lifetime cash flow forecast illustrated that she could afford to spend her capital, as long as she downsized her property by her late 80s.

Going one step further Sally actively sought out properties that she would happily move in to at that stage of life, to fully appreciate the financial implications, which were built in to her cash flow projections. Knowing today where she could afford to live in years to come removed some of the worry about making this major decision later in retirement.

For further financial peace of mind, Sally created an additional income stream by renting a room in her house to foreign students during the summer months.

As a result, Sally no longer worried about whether her assets would support her desired retirement, and instead got on with enjoying her time with family. Renting the room also provided Sally with regular social interaction in her retirement, which she admitted she really valued.

Expert view

We interviewed Suzy Miller, The Alternative Divorce Guide who helps people navigate their way through the divorce process in a way which saves them money, protects the children and keeps them out of court.

Suzy runs the Alternative Divorce Guide Directory at www.alternativedivorcedirectory.co.uk which helps guide people towards creating a solid plan of action when getting divorced.

Ready, Steady, Retire!: How are the post-war generation approaching the subject of divorce and separation?

Suzy Miller: There's a whole generation now of older people who don't have quite such a large taboo about staying together. There's more freedom for people to make choices.

To be blunt, a lot of women in particular just get to a certain age and think, "Is this it?" and realise that they do have a choice, especially if their adult children have already been through divorce.

Having said that, it's an incredibly difficult thing to do particularly if you're financially settled. It's always a big financial decision to make to split.

Ready, Steady, Retire!: The statistics seem to suggest that as many men as women are likely to initiate divorce. Does this match your experiences with clients?

Suzy Miller: Yes, I think men are just as likely to initiate a divorce later on in years as the women. At that point in people's lives, they are both looking forward and thinking, "What's it all about?"

There are plenty of older men who find that they can - especially if they've been successful in their business - trade in for another wife, a younger model, as they say. They're still on perhaps a different journey to their wives who've been spending all their time with the children.

Couples have simply grown apart. I can understand why there would be a fairly 50/50 split with the men and the women and the older age group.

Ready, Steady, Retire!: We often think about the impact of divorce on younger children, but when it comes to 'silver splitters', do we still need to be thinking about the impact on their adult children?

Suzy Miller: When I was at a talk a while back with older people, grandparents many of them, I really reiterated that they need to be very careful when they're going through breakup from their children's point of view. Often if their children have gone through their own divorce or breakup, they'll have a tendency to take sides and then wonder why they don't get to see the grandchildren.

Understanding things like mediation, and collaborative law, and the stay-out-of-court options is really, really important for everyone, but particularly for an older age group. Not only for when their own children break up and they want to keep relationships as sweet as possible so they can keep a relationship with their grandchildren, but also for themselves when they themselves go through divorce and separation.

There's so many ripples out from that experience which would cause so much damage still. Even adult children get very, very upset when their parents break-up and divorce. It's very, very challenging. It's vital that those people take steps to make sure it doesn't end up a nasty battle in court.

One of the main reasons for really striving for non-adversarial divorce, particularly for the older age group, is that they don't want to lose all that money that they built up over the years painstakingly on lawyers' fees.

But as importantly, they don't want to cause havoc in their family lives with children siding with parents. It can be quite horrific what can happen.

I would always advise everyone, but in particular that the older generation who are going through divorce or breaking up, to access mediation, to find out about collaborative law, which they may never have heard of, but keeps them out of court.

Ready, Steady, Retire!: To what extent did the global financial crisis, starting in 2007, and subsequent economic recession influence decisions to divorce among the Baby Boomer generation?

Suzy Miller: I feel that with the difficult times that we've had with the recession that money can certainly be a trigger for divorce particularly for the old age group. Though some may seem very financially settled, others have really struggled and businesses have gone down. Sometimes that financial instability has been the final straw in being a catalyst for that relationship to completely collapse.

Even for those who've managed to stay financially stable during the recession, they certainly don't want to be putting their wealth at huge risk through an acrimonious divorce. I would feel it's a great shame if people who've worked so hard for the assets they have they want to hand them on to their children, spoil that by letting emotion and bitterness perhaps, years of bitterness in some cases, come bubbling up.

These are very natural things in divorce which is why it's so important that people seek well-being help, not just counselling, but coaching, anything that's going to help put them emotionally and psychologically in the right space to be able to deal with the crisis that's going to be a lot harder than they probably realise.

Ready, Steady, Retire!: Is it fair to say that the older generation tend to be less impulsive when it comes to separation and divorce, than perhaps younger people are sometimes considered to be?

Suzy Miller: I think it's fairest to say that divorce in the older generation is less impulsive than perhaps we consider the younger generation to be. Personally, I don't think divorce is ever very impulsive at all. It's incredibly difficult, particularly if you have families.

One of the benefits that the older generation have, having in general thought it through very carefully, is that their children are often older, which doesn't mean it's not still difficult. It certainly frees up the mother usually enormously to make such a drastic decision.

I feel that it's very often the case perhaps that there's infidelity touted as the reason. I tend to think that's often just a catalyst. I don't think it's the sole reason why a solid relationship over years and years would split just because one or other of them are having a bit of a mid-life crisis. It tends to be a very carefully thought out decision that they make.

I would hope that being older and wiser, that they would also seek out a really wide holistic range of experts and not just think of running to a lawyer and trying to grab as much of the household wealth as they can.

I always encourage people to seek a very wide range of advice from well-being, financial advice in particular, and as well as mediation or collaborative law if they want that lawyer to be by their side through the process. Under no circumstances should they simply head to court. Just because the children are older doesn't mean you can't cause a lot of friction and unhappiness in the family as a whole which is not what you want in your later years. You want peace at the end of the day.

Ready, Steady, Retire!: When people enter their fifties and sixties, their lives often change quite dramatically, with many parents suddenly experiencing empty nest syndrome, as the children leave home. Does this contribute to the rise of the silver splitter?

Suzy Miller: Yes, empty nest syndrome is a very real phenomenon. You can prepare for it though.

I feel that some of the best things that women in particular can do is as the kids get older, rather than just hanging on to their children's every drama or music performance, they need to be building up another life for themselves.

That can be taking up singing, joining sports groups, or even starting a new part time business from home. These are the kind of things I actually encourage people to do when they're going through divorce. They really help re-build self-confidence, and give people direction, and help them to look forwards to what they want to create in their lives.

I've seen through this divorce arena quite often people will come along to me and they will want information. They feel they're definitely going to get divorced. Once they've sorted out their finances, taken responsibility for their lives, started to look forward, quite often they find it's not the relationship that's the problem, it's them.

By pre-empting an empty nest syndrome, by making sure you are rebuilding your self-confidence, creating direction in your life, you're far less likely to have issues with your relationship as a whole.

For the men, empty nest syndrome affects them also.

Suddenly their wife wants more attention than they were perhaps used to. They were used to having a lot of independence quite often. Suddenly that all changes. They also can prepare for that in the same way they would prepare for retirement by making sure they've got busy, active lives and are fulfilled. If you've got two happy fulfilled people, together they tend to get on quite well I find.

Ready, Steady, Retire!: Divorce in later life can often result in loneliness, which is a growing problem for retirees these days. Can you prepare for this and do something about it?

Suzy Miller: One of the saddest things I hear about in our country today is how many people, particularly older people live completely alone, have very limited social lives; especially physically they start to ail. They can't go out so easily. They become very, very isolated.

That is again something you can really prepare for. It's vital that people look around in their community and make the most of it.

I go to local events in my village which have people in their 80's dancing and having a dance with friends, right through to local film societies where people gather together. There's many things that people can do either as couples or independently. That's quite important.

Older people often will get used to hanging on each other's coat tails when it comes to going out and doing things. Really, they should be developing a real independence as early as possible and not rely on each other to go out and about and to do nice things. You've got more to talk about when the other one comes home. You shouldn't have to just do all the same things together just because you're married.

Ready, Steady, Retire!: Has the cultural history of the Baby Boomer generation influenced their attitudes towards divorce and separation in later life?

Suzy Miller: I definitely think that the older people now have had more of a youth than perhaps their parents did or more of an exciting time when they were young in the sense of more experimentation.

However sensible they may seem now, they've often had quite a wild past.

When people get older, particularly if they're having a bit of a mid-life crisis, they remember that wild past and they want more out of life. People these days have very high demands on what they feel they should get from life especially if they're looking back at the past with rose-coloured glasses.

They just have a greater confidence about independence. I know quite a few older people that look back with fondness at when they were single years and years ago. There is an idea that they're somehow restricted when they're in a relationship because he doesn't like her doing this or she doesn't like him doing that, which I think is a great shame.

Of course that is not really true. People use these excuses without realising it is an excuse to keep themselves stuck. They become afraid. They become so used to only doing things with someone else like only going out socially when they're with their husband or their wife. I would recommend whether someone's going to stay in the longest marriage ever or break up that they do practice independence by going out on their own.

For someone older in the Baby Boomer generation, it's a massive challenge, so practice early and often. Create your own social life really. Don't try to always be doing the same thing as the other partner.

Ready, Steady, Retire!: If Baby Boomers are considering divorce, where can they turn for reliable information?

Suzy Miller: When people are even considering getting a divorce or splitting up, I think quite often now they're going on the Internet. They need to be very careful. There's lots of advice there, but not always coming from a voice that's encouraging them to be non-adversarial, stay away from court. It can be very overwhelming.

I believe if people get the information they need very quickly and very clearly, then they're able to make a more informed decision. Sometimes by getting the right information, people will sort out perhaps their financial issues and they won't need to get divorced at all. Others will decide it is the best thing for their family as a whole in which case they realize that just running to a lawyer and asking them to fight their corner is a disastrous thing to do and totally unnecessary.

There are some fantastic choices out there. People just literally don't know it. If they come to me, I guide them towards the people who will give them the information they need, help keep them out of court, and help them make responsible decisions that are going to look at the long term, not just a short term fix of getting out of one relationship so they're free to have another one.

When people are in a state of pain, emotional pain, they often don't think clearly. It's really important to be guided. It's important to have someone tell you the truth, and tell you, perhaps, not always the things you want to hear, but guidance that's going to set you down a road that you really need to travel down.

In alternative divorce, which I would like to become the normal way of divorce, you don't go rushing straight for a lawyer. Yes, independent legal advice is important. That's just a tiny bit of the process. The key thing is to think of financial independence. I say to people, "Don't think about divorce, think about financial independence."

Thinking about financial independence means working with financial experts who have the training and skills to help you create a long term financial plan - that's not the lawyers' job.

Ready, Steady, Retire!: What's the most important help Baby Boomers need to seek when heading towards divorce? What help will result in the best outcomes for them?

Suzy Miller: Getting help with your heart and your mind is vital. Then you're in a stronger position to then deal with the financial side and the legal side and to keep it amicable. You've got your eye on where you want to be, which is not wasting your money, protecting the relationships with your children and the family and also protecting the relationship with your ex.

Even if things are nasty for a while and they're angry or upset, say there's been infidelity, it's amazing how a few years down the line if people do the right steps, that you can be at your daughter's wedding or your son's wedding and sit at the same table.

That should be the objective of anyone going through a divorce is to make sure that even if it seems impossible to imagine at the time that that's something that will be possible in a few years down the line.

Chapter Five
Squeezed Sandwich Generation

Squeezed Sandwich Generation

"Never lend your car to anyone to whom you have given birth." - Erma Bombeck

Another term for the post-war Baby Boomer generation is the 'sandwich generation'.

Squeezed by the financial and time pressures of adult children and elderly parents, increasing numbers of Baby Boomers have found themselves effectively sandwiched between the younger and older generation. This sandwich generation comes at a critical time in their own lives; just as they enter retirement.

Becoming a member of the sandwich generation is one implication of living longer; there is a greater chance you will experience a period of your life when you are caring for elderly parents and providing support in the form of money and/or your time to adult children.

According to Carol Abaya, a nationally recognised expert on the sandwich generation in the US, there are three different scenarios to consider.

The **traditional scenario** involves being sandwiched between ageing parents in need of care and helping your own children.

A club sandwich describes Baby Boomers who are in their 50s or 60s, squeezed between ageing parents and adult children or grandchildren.

The **open faced scenario** describes anyone else involved in caring for the elderly.

Whether you find yourself a part of the sandwich generation today, or you are likely to fall into one of these scenarios in the future, it is important to think about the impact this could have on your own plans for retirement.

Sandwiched women

Women more than men tend to find themselves squeezed between the demands of elderly parents and adult children.

IPPR research found thousands of women in their 50s are balancing work with care, or face being pushed out of work altogether; forced to take an early retirement because of their care obligations[44].

As many women wait until later in life to start families, the IPPR study into the sandwich generation found more than half of new mothers are relying on informal support from grandparents.

They found that grandmothers who provide this informal support are more likely to be in employment and belong to lower income households, which can make the consequences of providing this childcare support keenly felt.

Crowded houses

Being part of a sandwich generation is undoubtedly changing how Baby Boomers are living. Figures from the Office for National Statistics have shown a big growth in larger households; more than three million Brits are now living in homes with at least five other individuals.

The latest Census data for England and Wales identified at least 543,000 homes with at least six residents, making multiple occupancy households like this the fastest growing sector with a 25% rise in the past decade.

Often, these 'crowded homes' are the result of adult children continuing to live under the same roof as mum and dad. In 2013, there were 3.3 million adults in the UK between the ages of 20 and 34 continuing to live with one or more parents, representing a little over quarter of this age group still living at home[45].

These living habits can get expensive for parents. Research by insurer Engage Mutual found 46% of the parents of children over 25 years old continue to financially support their kids. This financial support comes in various forms, including clearing debts or paying for a deposit on a first property.

Later starts

With many parents choosing to start families later in life, there are consequences to consider for retirement planning.

In a traditional sense, the period of time when children have grown up and left home tends to be a prime opportunity to divert household expenditure towards retirement planning. Parents would usually wait until their children had flown the nest before feathering their own nests for later life.

Assuming you intend to retire on your 70th birthday, if your children have grown up and left home by the time you celebrate your 50th birthday, that gives you two solid decades of dedicated saving towards the cost of retirement.

This often coincides with lower household expenses - the mortgage has usually been repaid, or can be repaid quickly once University tuition fees are no longer leaving the family bank account each month - and a time when earning power is at its very highest. A combination of low expenditure and high earnings is ripe for saving for the future.

The trouble is, when families are being started later in life, children are not flying the nest until parents are well into their 50s, or 60s in some cases. This limits the financial opportunity to save for retirement, as the costs associated with raising a family stretch out into this prime time for boosting retirement funds.

Throw an unexpected event such as poor health or loss of employment into the mix, and it is easy to see how retirement planning can become totally derailed.

The only real solution to this challenge is to balance retirement planning with your other household expenditure throughout your working life.

Leaving it until your 50s and 60s to invest the bulk of your retirement funds is simply too risky and exposes your retirement planning to too many unknowns.

Caring employers

Being a part of the sandwich generation can also have an impact on your career prospects.

A recent survey found that one in three employers have experienced a rise in absenteeism due to their employees needing time to satisfy caring responsibilities. The Chartered Institute of Personnel and Development (CIPD), along with medical provider Simplyhealth, found more people are taking time off work to provide childcare or to care for elderly relatives.

An estimated three million employees in the UK are juggling employment and their duties as a carer, either as a parent or delivering care to ageing parents. This is estimated to cost businesses around £3.5bn a year[46].

Despite the growth in members of the sandwich generation, many employers appear poorly prepared for the phenomenon. Only one in six employers report having policies in place to help their employees balance caring responsibilities with their work.

The CIPD is encouraging bosses to put in place formal policies which will support members of the sandwich generation, for the ultimate benefit of business.

Allowing staff a more flexible approach to work could help defer retirement and retain talent in companies for longer.

In addition to flexible working arrangements, employers can help support employees who are part of the sandwich generation by allowing compassionate leave, paid or unpaid carer's leave, access to counselling services and career breaks. Rather than losing valuable employees because of their caring responsibilities, employers could retain quality staff by implementing these policies.

Balancing the karmic scales

Of course being a part of the sandwich generation is not all bad. With the right planning, many of our clients report how pleasurable it is to have the opportunity to spend time with elderly parents.

For these more fortunate members of the sandwich generation, it is a privilege to give back to parents the care they so happily provided earlier in life. Like repaying an emotional debt, caring for elderly parents in the later stages of their life can often feel like balancing the karmic scales.

Giving adult children a helping hand onto the property ladder or clearing expensive debts on their behalf can also be a very rewarding experience. When we speak to clients who decided to offer financial assistance to their children, they enjoyed being able to do this during their lifetime, rather than the money cascading down the generations as an inheritance following death.

Gifting wealth during life places parents in greater control of the money and allows them to see how it directly benefits their children or grandchildren, rather than feeling like a distant event written in a Will.

Caring for grandchildren also forms an important part of the retirement plans for many. This valuable service for the benefit of adult children saves expensive childcare costs and allows careers to flourish at an important stage in life, whilst maintaining strong family relationships. Assuming they are not treated as unpaid babysitters and children appreciate the value of the time that is being provided, it can be a great reciprocal arrangement.

What drives the quality of these relationships is an open and honest dialogue. Caring arrangements which come about by accident and are taken for granted often result in resentment, feeling like a burden to the person providing the care.

Talking about expectations, boundaries and plans helps to avoid any feelings that one generation is being taken advantage of. These can be difficult conversations, particularly if you feel unable to provide as much care as elderly parents or adult children need, or if you want to prioritise your own leisure time over and above the provision of care.

Often being a part of the sandwich generation will require careful balancing of the needs of the three (or more!) different generations; considering the implications of what one generation requires on the life of another. This can require a great deal of flexibility, particularly as needs change over time.

Case Study – Squeezed sandwich generation

Max was 56 years old and Michelle recently celebrated her 54th birthday. With their children recently leaving the family home after graduating from University, both were looking forward to a period of lower expenditure combined with strong earnings from Michelle's career as a well-paid management consultant and Max's work in the charity sector.

This was their opportunity to boost savings for a decade or so before they stopped work to enjoy a long and hopefully healthy retirement. Both admitted to having lower than desirable levels of pension savings, with other financial demands taking priority during their careers to date.

However, the mortgage on their family home had been recently repaid and the capital value of an investment property purchased 15 years ago had skyrocketed in recent years as the economy improved, albeit with a hefty interest-only mortgage attached.

Within the space of a couple of months, a series of unexpected events happened at once. Their son, Robert, went through a bitter divorce which resulted in him losing his matrimonial home. Wanting to support their son, Max and Michelle agreed to use 80% of their savings to get him straight back on the property ladder, effectively investing in a new property alongside their son but waiving any rent to help him reduce his outgoings.

Shortly afterwards, Michelle's father died suddenly leaving her mother alone and quickly unable to cope. Michelle's 82 year old mother had been struggling for years with the early stages of dementia along with several other medical conditions which left her reliant on her husband for daily support.

With that support suddenly gone, Max and Michelle took the difficult decision for Michelle to take a sabbatical from work and become her mother's full-time carer.

With retirement plans in turmoil, we met with Max and Michelle to help them develop a plan to suit their new membership of the sandwich generation. The first step was establishing their true financial position, which turned out to be much better than they originally thought, once legacy pension assets and state benefits were taken into account.

The Financial Plan we developed for Max and Michelle was used to illustrate a range of scenarios, showing them that they could afford for Michelle not to return to work and still afford to maintain their lifestyle in retirement, assuming a few tweaks were made to their investment strategy.

Options to sell the investment property, eventually sell out of their interest in Robert's new house and even downsize their own home were all considered, and plans for each option were formulated.

Max and Michelle finished the Financial Planning process with the peace of mind that everything was going to be OK, regardless of how long Michelle's mum needed her care.

Chapter Six
Defining Diseases

Defining Diseases

"The Baby Boomers are getting older, and will stay older for longer. And they will run right into the dementia firing range. How will society cope?" - Terry Pratchett

There's a downside to living for longer. With improved longevity comes a greater propensity for age-related diseases, in particular dementia.

Dementia has no cure and describes a set of symptoms which include memory loss. There are various causes, including Alzheimer's disease which is the most common cause of dementia. Research in the US has found that the average life expectancy for someone diagnosed with dementia is eight to ten years[47].

Alzheimer's has been called the defining disease of the Baby Boomer generation. Cases of dementia in the UK are forecast to rise to 1.5m by 2020, from their current level of around 800,000[48].

By 2050, around two million Britons are expected to suffer from Alzheimer's according to the Alzheimer's Society, who recently commented on the "staggering financial and human impact" of dementia on the country.

225,000 people each year are developing dementia in the UK, with one new diagnosis every three minutes of the day.

However, less than half of people with the disease will receive a diagnosis, so the real scale of the dementia epidemic is likely to be far greater.

Dementia is a disease which tends to afflict older people. For every five year age group, the proportion of people with dementia doubles. Put simply, the older you get, the greater the chance you will have dementia. At age 95, over a third of people have dementia.

Women tend to have dementia to a greater extent than men, probably because they tend to live longer lives. Two-thirds of dementia cases are found in women.

Amongst those living in residential care homes, nearly two-thirds have been diagnosed with dementia, making this one of the leading reasons prompting a need for residential care in later life.

What is dementia?

Dementia is a collection of symptoms, rather than a specific disease itself. It refers to the loss of mental functions including thinking, memory and reasoning, to the extent that it interferes with daily living.

Alzheimer's Disease is one of the most common causes of dementia. This causes the loss or degradation of nerve cells in the brain, falling into the same category of diseases as Huntington's and Parkinson's Disease.

However, there are around 50 other diseases and infections which can cause dementia, some of which are very rare.

Strokes, for example, affect blood vessels in the brain. Dementia can also be caused by reactions to drug or alcohol use, nutritional deficiencies, infections of the brain and spinal cord, or head injuries.

There is a big difference between symptoms of ageing and symptoms of dementia. Getting older can often result in forgetfulness or being easily distracted. Difficulty in retrieving information - the feeling that a word is 'on the tip of my tongue' - can also just be a part of old age.

Symptoms which indicate dementia tend to be more serious, having a disruptive effect on your ability to live independently or carry out activities of daily living.

This can include difficulties in carrying out simple tasks, struggling to make simple choices, or getting disorientated in familiar locations. If you or a family member start to display symptoms like this, it is always worth getting checked out by a GP.

In some cases, dementia can cause changes to moods, personality and behaviour.

The cost of dementia

Dementia is an expensive business, for society, individuals and their families. In the UK alone, the financial cost of dementia is estimated to be around £26bn a year.

Because of the sterling work carried out by families to care for people with dementia, it is estimated that over £11.6bn a year is saved for the taxpayer. Carers of those with dementia are left with these costs as they spend 1.3bn hours a year providing this unpaid care for everyday tasks including washing and dressing.

Dementia UK found that over a third of the cost associated with dementia was due to unpaid care delivered by family members, friends and other volunteers. This does not however include the amount of lost income for carers who have to give up work early or start working on a part-time basis. Lost income for those caring for people with dementia is estimated at around £690m a year[49].

These headline figures are often quite meaningless in the context of the financial cost to individuals and their families. In 2012, Dementia UK calculated that the average cost to each of the 800,000 people in the UK living with dementia was around £29,746.

This average cost varied depending on the severity of the dementia and the residential setting for the person involved. For individuals living in the community with mild dementia, the annual cost was an average of £14,450. For people with dementia in a residential care home, the average cost was a far greater £31,263 each year.

Where people with dementia require residential care, a large element of the cost (over 40%) is for accommodation.

For Baby Boomers who have carefully planned a comfortable retirement, the arrival of dementia can quickly decimate savings and place a real financial pressure on resources; both time and money.

Ways to prevent dementia

Government guidelines suggest a number of measures Baby Boomers can take which will reduce their risk of developing dementia in later life.

- Eating a healthy diet.

- Maintaining a healthy weight.

- Exercising regularly.

- Not drinking too much alcohol.

- Stopping smoking (if you smoke).

- Keeping your blood pressure at a healthy level.

These are all sensible suggestions, not only for maintaining a good cognitive function in later life, but for maintaining good overall physical health.

Other steps you can follow have less scientific backing, but could still help to stave off damage to your brain cells and keep your mind healthy in retirement.

Eating foods rich in antioxidants - blueberries, broccoli and tomatoes are good examples - can help to slow the development of dementia. Dark chocolate, which contains high levels of an antioxidant called flavanols, is another good tip.

As our expert Jennifer Rusted goes on to explain later in this chapter, building a bigger brain (and therefore a larger cognitive window) is an important strategy for limiting the symptoms caused by brain damage; lifelong learning is a good way to grow a bigger brain. Keeping your mind active and engaged is likely to help prevent, or at least slow down, dementia.

While the official government guidelines recommend not drinking too much alcohol, some studies have found that drinking red wine in moderation can help protect the brain. Consuming small amounts of alcohol can be anti-inflammatory and raises levels of good cholesterol in the body. Red wine in particular is praised for its high levels of antioxidants.

The obesity link to dementia seems reasonably well supported, with one study finding that obese people have 8% less brain tissue than people with a healthy weight. Overweight people who are not yet obese were found to have 4% less brain tissue.

Good sleep is another important preventative strategy, with a lack of sleep generally toxic for brain cells.

As Baby Boomers continue to age, we expect to see more work done on finding ways to prevent dementia and even developing more effective treatments. It is set to become something which inflicts more Baby Boomers than any other generation, so taking steps as early as possible to protect against the impact of dementia is very important.

Planning for dementia

From a planning perspective, something that every Baby Boomer needs to put in place is a Lasting Power of Attorney (LPA).

This is a legal document which allows you to appoint one or more people (known as attorneys) to make decisions on your behalf, should you lose the mental capacity to make your own decisions.

There are two types of LPA to consider; Health and Welfare, and Property and Financial Affairs. Both types are equally as important for Baby Boomers to put in place.

The Health and Welfare LPA allows your chosen attorney to make decisions about your day-to-day activities, your medical care and even whether you should move into a residential care home. The Property and Financial Affairs LPA covers decisions about paying household bills, managing your bank account, collecting state benefits and even selling your home.

These are clearly big decisions and you must therefore only appoint someone as an attorney if you trust them to act in your best interests. When choosing a suitable attorney, think about how well they make their own decisions and manage their own finances. Clearly you do not want to appoint an attorney who is constantly exercising poor judgement or struggles with money decisions!

There are some protections in place to prevent attorneys from making decisions which would be detrimental to your wellbeing. When a Lasting Power of Attorney is registered, a notice of intention to register is sent to a list of people you have asked to be told, giving them an opportunity to raise any objections.

As the person subject to the LPA, you can object for any reason you like and you do not need to provide factual evidence to support this objection. Others can object to the LPA being registered on factual grounds, such as an attorney not having the mental capacity to act or being bankrupt.

An attorney must act in your best interests at all times, take reasonable care in making decisions and act in accordance with the terms of the Lasting Power of Attorney. This can vary depending on what you place in your LPA, but could include only being able to make decisions about 'life sustaining treatment' if the Health and Welfare LPA grants this specific power.

There is additional protection in the form of guidance contained within The Mental Capacity Act. This puts in place a framework for which decisions can be made under which circumstances, and contains the principle that every adult has the right to make his or her own decisions, and is assumed to have mental capacity unless it is proved otherwise.

We often find that Baby Boomer clients are reluctant to put a Lasting Power of Attorney in place due to the misconception it will allow others to 'rip them off' or make decisions contrary to their best wishes. In our experience, the combination of seeking legal advice and the safeguards contained within the process and Mental Capacity Act means there is nothing to fear from having a Lasting Power of Attorney.

In fact, it is a very sensible measure which avoids complex and often expensive legal wrangling should you lose mental capacity in later life without a Lasting Power of Attorney already in place.

To establish a Lasting Power of Attorney, you need to choose your attorney, fill in some simple forms and then register them with the Office of the Public Guardian, either immediately or when it is needed in the future. The process differs slightly in Scotland and Northern Ireland, but for Baby Boomers living in England it is really very straightforward.

Other health concerns

Of course dementia is not the only health concern for the Baby Boomer generation as they enter retirement and progress through later life. In our experience with Baby Boomer clients, this generation is increasingly concerned about various health risks and the impact these could have on their Financial Plans.

The 'big three' diseases are usually a pressing concern; heart disease, cancer and stroke. In Britain, we can add lung and liver disease to these killers. Combined, these are the five big killers which account for more than 150,000 deaths a year among the under-75s. Mortality rates from these big five rise sharply the older you get.

Coronary heart disease is the biggest killer, responsible for the deaths of around 200 people each and every day in the UK. Three-quarters of these deaths occur in the over-75s, as the risk of heart attack rises sharply with age. Smoking, being overweight and having high blood pressure are all risk factors.

Stroke is the third leading cause of death among the general population in the UK, responsible for the deaths of 150,000 people a year. Being able to spot the symptoms - which include facial weakness, difficulty speaking, and pins and needles down one side of the body - and then seeking urgent medical attention is vital.

Cancer is becoming so common in the UK that an estimated 1 in 30 are now either suffering from cancer or in remission[50]. There is a strong chance that someone in your family or someone you know has cancer. Medical advances have helped improve survival rates, along with earlier diagnosis, but unhealthy lifestyles continue to cause an estimated one-third of all cancer cases.

Liver disease is on the rise in the UK while it is falling in other European countries, largely prompted by our unhealthy approach to alcohol consumption. More than a third of men and a quarter of women drink too much each week; government guidelines are for no more than three or four units of alcohol a day for men and two to three units for women.

Blue Zone living

It's not all doom and gloom as the Baby Boomer generation reaches retirement and lives for longer than ever before. This improved longevity will undoubtedly be accompanied by growing health challenges. It also creates an opportunity for a very healthy retirement, as long as proactive steps are taken.

One source of inspiration comes from 'Blue Zones'. These are communities where common elements of lifestyle, diet, and outlook have led to an amazing length and quality of life. It is a concept used to identify a demographic or geographic area of the world where people are living longer and healthier lives.

The first Blue Zone was identified in Sardinia's Nuoro province, with the highest concentration of male centenarians living in this area of the country. Further Blue Zones have been found in Okinawa (Japan); Sardinia (Italy); Ni-coya (Costa Rica); Icaria (Greece); and among the Seventh-day Adventists in Loma Linda, California.

These Blue Zones share similar characteristics, which Baby Boomers can learn from in order to live longer and healthier lives in retirement.

- Family is put ahead of other concerns.

- There is less smoking.

- People follow a semi-vegetarianism diet. With the exception of the Sardinian diet, the majority of food consumed in these Blue Zones is derived from plants. Legumes are also commonly consumed.

- Constant moderate physical activity is an inseparable part of life. Get moving!

- Social engagement is a common theme, with people of all ages socially active and integrated into their communities.

By understanding and integrating these traits of Blue Zone living, Baby Boomers can improve their own health outlook in retirement and increase the chances of living fulfilling lives long into their 70s, 80s and beyond.

Case Study – Caring for an ill spouse

Janet and Peter were both suffering from Parkinson's' disease. Peter was caring for his wife, Janet, as she had become too ill to look after herself on a daily basis. Peter was well aware of how bad the situation was going to get.

Peter reached out to us and together we created a comprehensive plan, which included returning to their original home in Scotland, primarily for access to the free nursing care. This move provided valuable financial support for Janet's care, and in later years also for Peter's care.

Peter ended up predeceasing his wife, but by working with us to create a Financial Plan for his later years he had peace of mind that Janet would be financially secure and cared for as he wished her to be, whilst protecting much of the couple's assets. This had the added benefit of Peter being able to pass more of his wealth on to his son.

Case Study - Planning for care of an ill spouse in event of death

Hilary and Stephen were a successful couple who had just reached their respective 60th birthdays. They had recently finished putting their children through private education and planned to capitalise upon their healthy income years and squirrel money away for their retirement during their last five years of working.

As a successful yacht surveyor, supported by his wife on the report-writing side, Stephen had a high net worth client bank and would travel around the world surveying boats.

On turning 60, Hilary suffered a sudden stroke which left her very ill for over a year. Since then her recovery has been slow.

Five years later Hilary was still wheelchair-bound and unable to talk properly. As a result, Stephen became Hilary's full-time carer and was unable to continue running his business. The couple's plans of working for a further five years to fund their retirement were shattered.

Hilary and Stephen came to us looking for ways to address their concern of funding their retirement. It was also critical for Stephen to ensure that Hilary would be cared for in the event that he predeceased her.

We started by creating a lifetime cash flow forecast which incorporated their various incomings and outgoings, and a number of assumptions about how they would live in retirement, to illustrate what their financial future could look like.

Having worked through a number planning scenarios together, the couple realised that they could afford to fully retire, if they accessed their various pensions as advised to deliver the income flow needed.

We then went on to address the question of caring for Hilary in the event of Stephen's death. We went so far as to encourage them to identify a suitable nursing home where Hilary would be happy to live, if Stephen were no longer able to provide care.

With Hilary's life expectancy projected to be shorter than Stephen's it was also important to address whether he would be financially secure in the event of Hilary's death. A relatively large proportion of their income was from disability and caring allowances, but by discussing and building cash flow models of the couple's options, Stephen felt assured that by downsizing their home in later life he would remain financially independent.

Hilary and Stephen could then get on with living life as best they could, in the knowledge that their Financial Plan showed they would both be financially secure.

Expert view

Jennifer Rusted is a Professor of Experimental Psychology at the University of Sussex. Her research expertise includes behavioural neuroscience and cognitive decline with age.

We interviewed Professor Rusted to find out more about the outlook for dementia and other age-related diseases which will afflict the Baby Boomer generation in later life. Here is what she had to say:

Ready, Steady, Retire!: Rates of dementia seem to be growing rapidly as the population ages. What are the risk factors for the disease?

Professor Rusted: The biggest risk factor for dementia is ageing and as we can now treat physical illnesses and to keep people alive for longer we are inevitably going to have an increase in age related diseases. It's not just dementia; we have an increase in all age-related diseases, everything from strokes, Parkinson's Disease, anything that is more likely to affect people over 60 is increasing and dementia is just one of the them.

The longer we live, the more we are likely to experience dementia so over the age of 65 the risk is about 5% of individuals but over the age of 85 the risk of dementia is about 20%. There is an exponential rise in the risk for dementia as you age.

Ready, Steady, Retire!: What about genetic risk factors?

Professor Rusted: It's intriguing really because most people assume that there are genetic risk factors and there are, but genetic risk factors account for less than 1% of the dementia that we see. So in fact the majority of dementia is what's called sporadic dementia. That is, it is not inherited from parental genes.

There is one gene that does seem to be very heavily associated with dementia - that is the APOE4 gene. The Apolipoprotein E is a polymorphic protein that is associated with movement of cholesterol around the body. Each person has two different alleles of that APOE gene and there is one particular allele or genetic variant that is highly associated with the risk of dementia and that is the APOE4.

Around 15% of the population carry an E4 allele and carrying any E4 will increase your risk for dementia around fourfold. And carrying two E4 will increase your risk even more.

So it's not an inherited gene, it's not a genetic link like familial dementia but its associated with increased risk and it's probably because it interacts with the other factors that we know precipitate dementia.

Ready, Steady, Retire!: How long have researchers known about this risk factor? Is there work being done looking specifically at the APOE4 gene?

Professor Rusted: Researchers identified this risk factor in the 1980s, but we still don't know the details around what the connections are and that's part of the problem.

We know if you have an APOE4 gene you tend to age less well cognitively. You tend to have more of the proteins in the brain that are associated with dementia such as beta-amyloid and Tau and you also tend to have a greater likelihood of moving through to dementia independent of any other risk factors. It could mean you tend to get dementia earlier and experience it more severely.

With APOE, the problem is that it is neither necessary or sufficient to have an E4 allele. So, there is increased risk, a fourfold increase risk, but certainly there are a number of people who will have the gene of that variation and not get dementia. So it's a difficult kind of balance between informing individuals about the increased risk and stressing or distressing them about the possibilities that it's going to increase their risk because it's not inevitable, that's one of the problems with dementia.

Ready, Steady, Retire!: So dementia isn't inevitable, even with the presence of this APOE4 gene which 15% of the population have?

Professor Rusted: It's not inevitable, you can age really well, it's not just about ageing it's about a whole pathological series of things that happen in the brain; some people get it and some people don't.

Some people with an APOE4 gene don't get it and others do. So the APOE4 gene is interesting because we do know it correlates with lots of the other risk factors for dementia. On the other hand it's not a topic that's really generated much beyond correlations at the moment.

Ready, Steady, Retire!: It's fair to say that dementia is a pretty complicated disease then?

Professor Rusted: Dementia is really complicated and is not a single disease. There's a lot of different types of dementia that we are learning more about, and how many different syndromes there are. We are certainly learning more about different forms of dementia but we're also recognising that each individual is very different which makes finding a cure very difficult.

We also know that dementia is about a cascade of effects that are probably precipitated by changes to the brain that happen very early, perhaps before the age of 30, but certainly before the age of 50. This is when you start seeing changes in the brain.

The issue is how we intervene and how we can understand what precipitates the negative cascade in some individuals where other individuals just carry on quite successfully through old age without those changes and we really are not close to knowing what precipitates dementia.

We know a lot about what dementia looks like when people have it but we don't know for sure what triggers it. So there's been a lot of interest looking at risk factors and we can understand things that protects against it, but the issue of what triggers it is ultimately nowhere near being answered.

Ready, Steady, Retire!: What steps can Baby Boomers take to reduce the risk of dementia in later life?

Professor Rusted: There is an awful lot literature out there that tells you good things that you can do and these are reasonably well supported.

Exercise has an effect because we know that the brain is simply an organ really like the rest of the organs in the body.

If you have a good cerebral vascular system and if you are engaging the brain properly by supplying it with good nutrients and ensuring that the brain can eliminate all its by-products effectively, in other words by having a good vascular system that feeds nutrients and removes the by-products, then that's a really good thing to do. Exercise promotes good brain vascular coverage and healthy vessels.

A healthy diet - putting the right things into your body and hoping that the brain uses them properly - is another really good way to protect the brain.

We also know cognitive stimulation that asks the brain to work hard and challenges the brain to do stuff is really effective, ensuring the brain optimises its capacity, like the old Sudoku puzzles and stuff like that.

The other factor that we know is important is social environment; social stimulation is good and social isolation is a risk factor for many age related diseases. It's definitely the case that living alone and living unsupported is a risk factor for many things.

Ready, Steady, Retire!: Regular exercise, a healthy diet, cognitive stimulation and a good social environment can all help reduce the risks of dementia, then. Are there any other strategies that Baby Boomers can follow as they enter retirement?

Professor Rusted: The other factor which we know a bit about which is quite interesting is called cognitive reserve and that's about putting in place a long term strategy to look after your brain. A really good cognitive reserve provides the brain with the capacity to deal with the disease related changes that happen with dementia; people who have the same biological damage will experience quite different symptoms depending on how good their cognitive reserve is. It's a bit like having a biological window and some people have a big window so that they can actually sustain quite a lot of damage without showing symptoms and others have a very small window so any small amount of damage will result in the expression of symptoms.

That's something which we think is probably building up all your life; you can sort of add to your cognitive reserve all your life.

That's why social environment, cognitive stimulation, physical exercise and diet are all really good things to engage in from a very early age because the earlier you engage in those the better your cognitive reserve and the better basis for sustaining good brain activity even in the presence of these biological changes that are happening.

Ready, Steady, Retire!: How much progress is being made towards developing a cure for dementia? Is this an area where pharmaceutical companies are spending a lot of money?

Professor Rusted: If you look at the amount of money that has gone into cancer - this is always a comparison that's made - with the money that's gone into dementia, it is very, very small.

The difficulty is that the money that has gone into dementia has not produced positive outcomes and so we have a situation where we have to really re-think the strategy of what we are using that money for.

Drug companies have put around $30 billion into developing drug treatments for dementia and those treatments are not really very effective, because they are aimed at people who are experiencing the symptoms already and therefore have quite severe brain damage. They don't arrest the brain damage, they simply treat the symptom which means their efficacy is quite low and the costs are quite high.

The benefits to some people of these drug treatments can be quite significant. Some individuals do experience benefits but in the majority of individuals the benefits are very small. So the strategy of targeting the disease once it's already in place is probably the wrong one because the drugs produced so far are not disease modifying in any way.

Ready, Steady, Retire!: Where do you think resources for dementia research should be focused?

Professor Rusted: Much, much less money goes into issues of care and resources for taking care of people who have dementia. We really want a quick fix that's the trouble, we want something that we can give people with dementia that's going to make them function better and show less symptoms and that's still really unlikely to happen.

So maybe we should be putting our resources into developing more effective systems of care that we can put in place for people who have dementia and focussing on trying to look for drug treatments that would prevent the onset of the damage. There are drugs in production that are supposed to be looking at that end of things. Immunisation, for example.

A couple of drugs that are under development were tested in humans to immunise against the build up of the kind of proteins that we think precipitate the cascade of events. They haven't really proved to be effective but you know we should be looking at much earlier interventions. This is a very long way off.

If we are going to really do anything about people who are moving through to dementia now, what we have is a massive problem of how we care for the people who, even if they're asymptomatic at the moment, they are too far into the process not to develop a dementia. So we were looking at the tip of the iceberg really.

We have a lot of people who are in their 40s, 50s, 60s, for whom it's already written that they are going to get dementia and we are not going to be able to do anything drug wise, therapeutically, to intervene.

Ready, Steady, Retire!: Compared to other age-related diseases, stroke and cancer for example, dementia sounds a long way behind the curve?

Professor Rusted: We are very good at keeping people alive. We are very good at stroke and getting even better with cancer. As our ageing population increases we are going to see a higher number of people with dementia and living with dementia.

One of the key buzzwords at the recent G8 Dementia Summit was 'living well with dementia'. This is what we should be thinking about; not trying to prevent people from getting dementia or try to cure dementia because we can't. We just don't know how to do that. What we should be focusing on is 'living well with dementia'

At the G8 Dementia Summit they announced a number of initiatives. David Cameron announced a number of initiatives around trying to develop a better understanding of the resources that are needed and the relationships to encourage 'living well with dementia'.

That's a focus on the person with dementia, which is all well and good, but people around that dementia need to be looked after too and any support we can give to them will have good knock on effects for the person with dementia.

So it's about who is going to care for that person with dementia and if they aren't caring for that person with dementia then the state will need to care for them. So in fact it isn't just one person that's affected it's a whole family that is affected. And that whole family needs care and support.

Focusing on how we best use the resources that we have got socially, psychologically, financially, economically and how we put that together in a package that best supports the people who are going to be doing the caring is a new and real challenge. That may well be family but it may be that social services and so on are best positioned to help.

Ready, Steady, Retire!: It sounds like we need to approach dementia in a different way to other age-related disease?

Professor Rusted: We definitely need to look at it in a different way and make sure we are optimising all those resources. We are currently depending on caring from unpaid volunteers and family members and it's not appropriate at all to ignore their input and their needs and just be focusing our efforts on trying to make a drug that's going to sort it, because it's not going to happen.

It's not going to happen for the next 20 years because nothing is out there that's even at the phase one development yet, that's looking more promising than the 20 years of dementia drug development failure that we experienced so far.

The first drug for dementia was licensed 40 years ago and the most recent one 14 years ago. Both are exactly the same family, based on the same pharmacology, so we haven't got any new ideas on how to do what is needed. The fact that actually nothing has come through and produced effective treatments is really rather frightening.

Chapter Seven
The Toll of Old Age Care

The Toll of Old Age Care

"Be nice to your kids. They'll choose your nursing home." - Abraham Maslow

One consequence of living longer but not necessarily healthier lives is the greater propensity to require care in later life. The need for care in your own home (known as domiciliary care) or care provided in a residential care home grows with age.

As things stand in the UK, around 420,000 adults currently receive residential care[51]. One in five people over the age of 70 receive care in their own homes, and 20% of these individuals with domiciliary care are receiving this on a continuous basis.

It's a sad fact of life that many of us will be unable to look after ourselves unaided in our old age.

Care is often required when an older person becomes physically or mentally ill, or when they suffer a disability which makes carrying out activities of daily living too challenging. These events can mean you become unable to perform basic tasks such as washing or dressing yourself.

Changing social structures mean the old days of families providing care to elderly relatives are now impractical in many cases. Different family dynamics mean adult children are often unable or unwilling to devote several years to caring for elderly parents, which results in having to consider other sources of help.

Whether you opt for care at home or residential care when that time comes, it can be a seriously expensive business. Our clients are often shocked by just how expensive care is to deliver, with financial assistance from local authorities reserved for those with the most limited financial means.

As a rough guide, it can cost up to £30 an hour to receive care in your own home. This quickly adds up to £1,800 a month for someone needing only a couple of hours a day of personal assistance at home.

If you need residential care, the best quality care homes charge upwards of £1,200 a week for the privilege. There are big regional differences in the cost of care, with homes in London and the South East charging even more.

With such expenses, assets can be quickly depleted as the shortfall between income and expenditure is covered.

Who pays for care?

In simple terms, if you can afford to pay for your own care in retirement, you will be the one who pays. Financial assistance from the state is means-tested based on the level of your assets. In England currently, this means that if you have assets exceeding £23,250, you will have to fully fund your own long-term care costs, at least until your wealth runs dry and the local authority has to pick up the tab.

With the average property price in the UK at around £250,000, those who own their house will usually be expected to fully fund their own care costs. The expectation is there that you will sell your home to pay for long-term care.

Property is not always included in the means testing for care funding. Property will be disregarded by your local authority if someone else who is eligible to do so continues to live there when you require residential care. This can include your spouse or civil partner, a relative who is at least 60 years old, a disabled relative, or a dependent child under 16 years old.

If none of the above applies, your property is generally disregarded for a period of twelve weeks. During this time the local authority will make a contribution towards your care costs, effectively loaning you the money to pay for care.

In some cases you might be eligible for the NHS to pick up the tab, under an arrangement known as Continuing Care. This is sometimes available when specific conditions are met, such as the individual needing care being unstable or unpredictable and requiring care around the clock.

If fully funded, this NHS Continuing Care can be provided in a residential care home, your own home, a hospice or elsewhere. In our experience, budget constraints mean it is very rare these days to be awarded Continuing Care in anything but the most serious cases.

What you should not expect to do in retirement is give away your wealth in order to qualify for local authority funding of your care needs. This is generally a bad idea, as local authorities treat cases of 'deliberate deprivation' very seriously, looking back through the history of any gifts you have made and seeking to restore your finances to their previous position, or treating you as if the disposal of wealth was never made in the first place.

Trying to make out that you have less financial resources also places you at the mercy of the state when it comes to the quality of the care you will receive. Having visited countless state run and private care homes, there is no comparison between the two.

Given the choice and means to pay for it, you will undoubtedly want to select your own care provider and not end up in local authority funded care, if you can possibly avoid it, and despite the high financial costs involved.

Other assistance

Safe in the expectation that you will be paying for your own care in later life, there are at least some other sources of financial assistance available to soften the blow.

An important benefit for those with long-term care needs is called Attendance Allowance. This is a non-means tested benefit which is available to those over age 65 who have care needs which last for longer than six consecutive months. It is currently paid at two rates, depending on whether you require care during the day or night, or continuously throughout the day and night.

If you are assessed as needing care from a Registered Nurse in a nursing home, you can receive an additional nursing care allowance known as Registered Nursing Care Contribution. This is another non-means tested and tax-free state benefit which is paid directly to care homes so they are reimbursed for any registered nursing care they provide.

These other forms of state assistance can all make a financial contribution to the cost of care, but it is unlikely to go far, particularly with the typical cost of a quality residential care home.

How to choose a care home

Choosing a residential care home can be a tricky business. It is often an emotional time, when the decision is finally made that a relative or loved one needs to move to a care home. Considering some of the following questions can help you choose the right home that suits their needs and of course your own requirements.

How far away is the home and will we be able to get there easily? Location of the care home is usually an important factor, as family will want to visit regularly.

If the family of the person needing care is spread across the country, you will need to decide whether to choose a central location accessible by all family members or somewhere local to one relative, perhaps someone who can accommodate other members of the family when they come to visit.

What facilities does the home offer? Depending on its location, the range of facilities offered within the home itself will be important to consider.

Care homes located within a town or village might rely on local facilities in the community, but those in more remote locations often seek to provide a wide range of facilities in-house. How far is it to the local shops, cafes and parks?

Does the home cater for all stages of care? A residential care home might cater perfectly for current care needs, but you also need to think about the future.

Some of the retirement villages we have visited recently address changing care needs by offering retirement housing, sheltered accommodation and a nursing home, all on the same site. This allows residents to move seamlessly between different services as their care needs change, without needing to relocate to a brand new home.

Are the other residents happy? You can tell a lot about the quality of a care home by spending some time with existing residents. Make time to visit a range of homes, and have a coffee and a chat with some of the existing residents, and also their families. Speak to the staff as well to get a feel for how they approach their work.

Is the care provider solvent? One of the biggest issues in recent years has been the financial strength of some private care home operators.

Before committing to a residential care home, always download the latest published accounts for the operator from Companies House. Look for the warning signs of debts and losses. Your chosen care home should be financially sustainable; this means they are profitable and are not attempting to service unmanageable debts.

Does the home allow pets? This can be a very important part of the decision-making process for some people. The ability to continue living with a beloved pet will sometimes make or break a move to a particular care home.

It might not be a pet; make sure the care home allows favourite hobbies such as art or woodwork to take place.

It's important to be very comfortable with your chosen residential care home. For this reason, we suggest people start the process of looking for the right care home a long time before the need to move there arises.

It is important to know where you wish to receive care in later life and, just as importantly, how that care will be funded. Make a plan and have it ready on a shelf to take down and put into action when the time arises.

Will current retirees change long-term care?

Just as they are changing the institution of retirement, we believe that the post-war generation who are retiring today will fundamentally change long-term care. In our experience from working with the leading edge of this generation, care provision is something which will need to become highly personalised, with a real service ethic attached.

Retirees are generally fearful of ending up in an institutionalised care home, with little to keep them active on a daily basis other than staring out of a window or participating in the occasional coach trip. Residential care providers in the future will need to cater for the specific requirements of individuals to a much higher standard than many have done to date.

In fact, our clients tell us that they want to avoid a move to a residential care home for as long as is possible. Instead, care provided in their own home is the preferred option. Assistance with daily activities such as preparing meals and cleaning is a more palatable option than leaving a familiar environment to live in a residential care home.

Moving into a care home can also mean giving up strong links to the local community. In the near future, we expect to see retirees take the issue of care in later retirement into their own hands, creating informal networks to provide support in the community.

Technology is also likely to play a big role in long-term care for the current generation of retirees. Cameras to aid assisted-living and prefabricated 'granny pods', backyard shelters which allow care to be provided in a family setting regardless of available space in the family home, are two technology innovations which already form part of the long-term care landscape.

Regardless of how long-term care changes, it is essential to plan for this eventuality rather than live with the false hope it will never happen to you. Explore the options for care in later life, chat to your family about your preferences (while you still have mental capacity) and consider the costs involved.

When or if the time comes when you require care, having taken care of the issues described in this chapter will undoubtedly make things go a lot more smoothly.

Case Study – Care decisions for an elderly parent

Barbara was enjoying her retirement with her husband, John, who suddenly died quite unexpectedly. Having never dealt with the family's finances before, Barbara found herself struggling to get to grips with what felt like very complex financial paperwork.

Barbara was introduced to us and we started by creating a Financial Plan tailored to her needs. Firstly we suggested she reorganise her assets to make them more easily manageable. By creating a life time cash flow we also worked out that Barbara had enough money to live on in her retirement and that she could afford to pass on some of her wealth to one of her sons at that point, rather than waiting until she passed away.

This was important to Barbara as she realised how beneficial the money would be to her son now, rather than at some point in the future.

Within twelve months, Barbara became seriously ill with cancer and quickly required full-time nursing care.

The issue of supporting his mother and finding appropriate care fell to Barbara's son, Tom, as he was the only family member living close by his mother.

Tom had already supported Barbara following the death of his father and helped her sort out her finances, whilst also coming to terms with the loss of his father. He now found himself helping support his mother through the diagnosis of her illness and her transition into residential nursing care, whilst running his own successful business and caring for his own family.

Barbara wished to stay in her own home but kept having falls, so Tom finally managed to encourage her to move into a residential nursing home. The huge amount of time needed to help his mother through this difficult period of her life, coupled with the emotional stress Tom has experienced have been incredibly testing.

As part of the Financial Planning process, Barbara put in place a Lasting Power of Attorney so that Tom could handle her financial affairs on her behalf, when she was no longer able to do so.

Case Study - Caring for elderly mother

Janine's mother was fit and healthy until she reached 90 years of age. She had to undergo a minor operation which involved having a general anaesthetic, which subsequently triggered the onset of dementia. Widowed for some years, her mother had been living alone at home successfully until this point, but gradually became more and more reliant upon Janine to care for her.

As she lived very near to her mother, Janine would visit every day. Over the following few months Janine found herself spending more and more time at her house, preparing every meal and providing intimate care. Janine even started staying at her mother's house, as she became unable to sleep alone.

Janine then suffered a fall herself, badly breaking her shoulder, which meant that her husband Nick had to step in and not only look after Janine's mother, but Janine too. They all ended up living at Janine's mother's house and Nick was providing the majority of the care. Janine's mother would not accept care from anyone other than her family, so they felt trapped in this arrangement.

Unable to go on holiday or live the retirement they had planned, Janine and Nick were stuck in the care trap for two years before Janine's mother passed away. If they had sought professional advice at the point Janine's mother first became ill, the stress the couple endured could have been mitigated to some extent.

Case Study - Financial security when ill

Fred had been in poor health for some time and his health was now rapidly deteriorating. Wheelchair-bound, he was starting to need full-time nursing care as his wife was no longer able to provide round the clock care on her own.

Fred was very aware of the pressure his care needs were placing on Margaret and he wanted to ensure that she wasn't stuck caring for him, unable to live her own retirement.

Early on, Fred made the decision to find somewhere to live out the rest of his years in comfort. He only expected to live for another couple of years, but ended up surviving for almost a decade longer.

At the time of finding a care home he was happy with, Fred came to us for advice and due to his severely reduced life expectancy we advised him to purchase an immediate care annuity, which was inflation-linked to ensure the income kept pace with price inflation. Alongside his state pension and other miscellaneous income from various sources, Fred managed to secure his care for the rest of his life.

With the finances sorted and secured, he was even able to continue contributing to his wife's housekeeping expenses, which was important for him to be able to do, despite Margaret not needing the income.

Fred lived in a lovely residential care home where he got along well with the staff and other residents. Margaret enjoyed visiting him each day, and subsequently he enjoyed his final years confident that Margaret was free to enjoy hers too.

Expert view

We met with Nigel Welby, executive chairman of Retirement Villages, a group committed to providing excellent homes and services so that residents can have all the benefits of home ownership, together with a first class quality of life within a sociable and supportive community.

Ready, Steady, Retire!: Where did the concept of retirement villages come from?

Nigel Welby: Well conceptually retirement villages started back in Victorian times when the great philanthropists created villages for their workers in their old age, so there's nothing novel about the idea within the not-for profit sector. But private retirement villages did start in the United States, and there's some very, very large retirement villages out there. Then they spread to South Africa, Australia and New Zealand. Only at a later date did they come over to the UK.

We own one of the first retirement villages in the UK at Cranleigh in Surrey, called Elmbridge Village. There are now quite a number of operators in the UK providing a range of retirement villages offering different types of services and accommodation.

Ready, Steady, Retire!: What is the purpose of a retirement village?

Nigel Welby: Well, what we are really trying to do is to create a quality of life. Everybody is going to live longer. We're going to numerically have many more years to enjoy. The difficult bit is making sure we do enjoy that. That's done two ways.

First of all the younger active retired people in their 60s and 70s will move in. This may not be where they would live 365 days a year. They downsize from the big family house moving here, they may well have a flat or a holiday home overseas they go to part of the year, and this is a lock up and leave solution. As they get older they can live here permanently in the village. The villages provide a range of services, of care services, of social services to support them into old age.

Now what distinguishes Retirement Villages from other types of specialist housing for the elderly such as shelter housing is that this isn't just if you like a block of flats with a warden and a lounge and somebody to do the gardening. The Retirement Villages essentially has a range of club house country club facilities like a golf club. There's a bar restaurant. There will be a medical clinic, a little shop, perhaps a snooker room, perhaps a spa, swimming pool.

It's a real five star hotel experience with a concierge service where people can be supported to liberate them from the drudgery of looking out the window and thinking, "the grass hasn't been mowed." It's to free them so they can use their time to the best of their ability.

They've had their eyes open to the art of the possible by their travels across the world, by the experiences they've had. It's in the same way as with schooling, for example, the modern generation of parent is much more demanding. You don't just drop your child at the school gate. Parents are now fully engaged, fully involved in what goes on in the school.

It's the same with retired people today. They're not prepared to tolerate just living where they've lived all their lives growing older. They want an active retirement. They want better quality facilities. This is one of a range of options. It wouldn't be right for everyone, but it's one of a range of retirement options to meet people's needs as they grow.

Ready, Steady, Retire!: What trends have you identified among the current retired population, when it comes to their accommodation needs in later life?

Nigel Welby: The first trend is there needs to be more retirement accommodation. The growth in the elderly population, nationally, the Office of National Statistics produced some statistics in May 2014 showing population trends over the 10 years to 2022. For the adult population the growth is about 2.6%. For those of us over 65 the population growth is 22.4%. I mean the difference is quite horrific.

The first question is, where are all those people going to live? Once upon a time in my parents' generation you had a job for life, you retired at 65, and if you did the decent thing, you shuttled off the end of the planet by the time you were 70. But now people are going to live to very old ages. Apparently I'm due to live to about 85, 90. My children who are in their 20s apparently are going to live to until they're over 100.

This puts enormous pressure on housing to start with as there will be a desperate shortage of housing. The people who move in to our villages move out of large family houses. It frees those houses up for younger families to move up into. So there is a desperate need just for more specialist accommodation for retired people.

I think the other trend is to keep our quality of life high there will be an increasing need for care for the elderly. Our villages can provide a range of care because, like the American villages, they're what's called continuing care retirement communities with a range of accommodations and service provision from active young retirees right to the people in their final months. That's a very humane way of looking after people in a community of their friends and their neighbours.

The other trend is in response to people becoming unpaid carers. I think at the moment 960,000 people in the UK are unpaid carers looking after a partner. That is going to rise substantially, probably more than double over the next 10 years. Our villages enable a couple to move in where one is a carer.

When they want a morning off we have a day care centre here where the infirm partner can be looked after. Or if somebody wants a holiday they can came in to our home for a couple of weeks.

Ready, Steady, Retire!: How are retirement villages tailored for the specific needs of the current retired generation?

Nigel Welby: What we try to do is to make the village not appear too tailored. The units look for all intents and purposes like a completely standard house or apartment you buy anywhere in the country. We try to pack them full of really high quality finishes and facilities. But discretely they are actually quite modified. In the kitchens for example the work tops are lowered, the cupboards are lowered, the oven is a special oven where the door folds back, the windows are electric. There's a whole range of subtle modifications.

There are emergency systems throughout every unit where people if they want can call for help. Most people actually when they move in the first thing they do is to disconnect all the emergency stuff. Then you find mysteriously a couple of year later they've switched the system back on again. Again, control is completely in the hands of the residents.

Of course we're not only looking after the residents here. We're also in many ways looking after their broader family. Because they have children. The children of our residents here will be in their 40s or 50s and they're very worried about mum and dad who are becoming older, who are becoming frail. So we're providing if you will a service to the entire family.

Ready, Steady, Retire!: When is the right time to consider a move into a retirement village?

Nigel Welby: Typically people keep in touch with us for a number of years before they make the purchase decision and sometimes they leave it until there is an event in their life. That event might be a heart attack, a stroke, a fall before the children very often decide that mum and dad need to be in a more sheltered environment. That really is a mistake.

Those who moved in when they were young enough to get the full benefit from the activities and the life of the village, they are the ones that get most out of this type of accommodation. So the best thing is if people can start to make that decision earlier.

Many of our residents are still working, because work now is not something that's just switched on or switched off. As you approach retirement people will ease off work, they will take part time jobs. A lot of our residents are still involved in the world of work. That's terrific.

So it's difficult to put a precise age, but certainly there's absolutely no reason why people shouldn't consider moving into these villages in their 60s. More typically they move in their 70s but it's a personal choice.

Chapter Eight
A Good Death

A Good Death

"I'm not afraid of death; I just don't want to be there when it happens." -
Woody Allen

It's often said that only death and taxes are inevitable in life. Facing up
to the realities of death and dying is an important part of the retirement
journey, despite our natural reluctance to consider end of life issues.

With longer lives and better standards of healthcare often comes delay
to the time when we need to address death. If anything, our collective
ability to keep people alive for longer has made end of life planning even
more important for retired people.

It creates better opportunities to consider what a 'good death' looks like,
often in relation to living a fulfilled life and leaving this planet with no
regrets. We can all agree that death is rarely 'good', but wanting to live
a long, happy and healthy life with minimal suffering or regrets when
the end comes can lead to a 'good death'.

What makes a good death?

Death is without doubt a very personal experience. Our views of dying
will often be shaped by our experiences of death throughout our
lifetimes; when family, friends or colleagues die, the experience will
usually inform our own views of dying and how it should be approached.
Social and religious attitudes towards death also play an important role.

There do seem however to be some shared attributes of what might be
considered a 'good death'.

Being in control of the process is something our retired clients tell us is
particularly important. There are often big decisions to be made towards
the end of life; how illnesses are treated, what medical intervention is
required or how a funeral should be organised. These are all factors that
we might wish to control or at least influence towards the end of our
lives.

Spirituality is also an important part of a good death for many, but not all, people. This can involve specific religious traditions or strong views about the exclusion of religion from the process of death and what happens in the time following death.

Our clients tell us that their greatest fear about death is the suffering. This can be their own suffering, with the wish to minimise pain or dragging out a serious illness through prolonged medical intervention. It might also be the desire to avoid the long-term suffering of those they love.

What many retired people hope to achieve before the end of their lives is closure; settling affairs in their final days, or preferably much earlier, so when the end arrives there are no regrets.

Regrets are also a key part of wanting to have lived a meaningful life. Dying with no regrets, or at least few regrets, must form part of a common wish list for a good death. This can take different forms; fulfilling relationships, raising happy children or making a difference to society are all common goals.

Parents first

Whilst planning for death is something that needs to be addressed during retirement, often it will be the death of one or both parents which acts as a catalyst for facing up to dying. With improved life expectancy, we are increasingly seeing the death of parents as members of the post-war generation first enter retirement.

"Death of a parent" has been a rapidly increasing search engine term over the past decade, as bereaved Baby Boomers look for resources to help cope with this situation. This can sometimes be the first close experience of death and the associated grief, making it harder to handle as it comes at a later stage in life.

Because the process of dying is very different today, often adult children will feel disconnected from the death of an elderly parent. Gone are the physical duties associated with tending to a parent on their deathbed, with hospitals or nursing homes commonly taking responsibility for this end of life care. As we become more distant from this final act, rationalising dying and planning for our own death can become more challenging.

At the same time, death has become more accessible than ever before. Morbid as it is, the Internet means that video clips of death are only ever a curious mouse click away. Television documentaries have done a thorough job of exploring the issues surrounding death and there are more public outlets than ever before to discuss dying.

Coffee, cake and death

Started in September 2011, the Death Café model offers a group directed discussion of death with no agenda, objectives or themes. People (often strangers) get together to eat cake, drink tea and talk about death. Their objective is to "increase awareness of death with a view to helping people make the most of their finite lives."

Death Café is a 'social franchise', which means anyone who signs up and follows their principles can host their own Death Café in the local community. Since they were formed, there have been over 1,000 Death Cafés held across Europe, North America and Australia. Don't be too shocked if you see one being advertised in your town or village in the near future.

The Death Café model was developed by Jon Underwood and Sue Barsky Reid, based on the ideas of Bernard Crettaz, a Swiss sociologist. Participants have different reasons for hosting and attending Death Cafes, but all are looking for an opportunity to openly discuss death, something we expect to see increase in the coming years.

In the US, a more popular approach is a discussion about death over a dinner party. The website deathoverdinner.org offers a guide for hosting a dinner party where discussing death is on the menu along with delicious food and drink.

By answering questions about who is coming to the dinner party and your intention for the evening, the website offers various resources to guide the discussions.

Whether your preferred outlet for important discussions like these is a Death Cafe or Death Over Dinner, our experience suggests the post-war Baby Boomer generation has a growing appetite for discussing death.

Getting practical

Grief aside, death has a real propensity to cause major financial issues. One of the most important things to do in preparation for dying is to be financially prepared. This can lessen the impact of death when it happens, avoiding unnecessary stress and conflict around the money issues created by a death.

You already know you need a will. This basic financial principle is drilled into all of us on a regular basis, with the implied message that it is irresponsible to die 'intestate' (without a valid will) as this means the state decides who gets your wealth.

Assuming you know you need a will and have actually done something about it, there are other important steps to take in addressing the practicalities of preparing for death.

We recommend starting with a summary of everything financial in one place. It is a great help to relatives, particularly your spouse or the executor of your will, to provide them with a regularly updated spreadsheet listing every financial asset you own. If you don't feel comfortable disclosing the details and values of accounts during your lifetime, at least ensure they know where to find the details when needed.

This spreadsheet should list bank accounts, pensions, investments and life assurance policies. Make life easier for loved ones by detailing account numbers and contact details. Some of our clients go to heroic lengths and even describe the death notification procedure for each product provider, in one case even compiling a file of pre-populated notification forms. Now that's thoughtful!

If you die without a financial summary spreadsheet, in many cases assets are overlooked and, in some instances, are lost forever. We have lost count of the number of occasions where bereaved spouses have presented us with boxes of paperwork, seeking our help in locating every financial policy from the piles of annual statements and policy documents.

Keep your financial summary along with a copy of your will, and make sure these can be located easily. Your significant other, the executor of your will, your solicitor and your Financial Planner should all know the location of these documents, ideally having their own copies on file for quick reference.

In addition to information, those you leave behind need knowledge. In Baby Boomer couples we usually discover that one partner, often the husband, has taken responsibility his entire life for managing the household finances and making important financial decisions.

When he dies, the transition for his widow can be overwhelming, having never taken an active interest in money matters. This can sometimes make the widow vulnerable or even unable to make important financial decisions, leading to inaction when action is required or an unwise course of action.

It is never too early – or too late - to start sharing financial responsibilities with your partner. Both husband and wife should know about every financial policy, how bills are paid and when household insurance policies expire.

This is my funeral

Funeral planning can form a very important part of discussions about death. It is more important to some than to others; we come across a variety of opinions from our clients when it comes to their funeral planning - some wish to plan every last detail down to the order in which their selected songs are played, others are content to delegate the responsibility of funeral planning to others.

Because of the variety of opinions out there about what the 'right' funeral looks like, it makes sense to at least offer your loved ones a little guidance during your lifetime. Aside from the fundamental decision of whether you wish to be buried or cremated, funeral planning can involve everything from the form of transport used, religious input to a service and the choice of flowers.

The individuality of the Baby Boomer generation means many are choosing to shun funeral traditions in favour of 'alternative' approaches. There is nothing hippie about wanting to have a natural burial, but as you will read later in this chapter in our expert view section, Baby Boomers are increasingly opting for a natural burial as they seek a connection to more traditional ways of managing the very final stage of their life.

With the growing view that our lives should be individual and personalised comes the desire to apply the same to funeral planning. Choosing a plot, selecting a bespoke coffin design and ensuring your favourite music is played; these are all options for those wishing to stamp their personalities on their funerals.

Wealthiest man in the graveyard

After working hard and saving hard your entire life, it is natural to be cautious when it comes to spending money. Being frivolous with cash is rarely second-nature to Baby Boomers, who in many cases have become wealthy in part due to a frugal attitude towards expenditure. But there is no sense in being the wealthiest man (or woman) in the graveyard.

Former Apple Inc. CEO Steve Jobs once said: "Being the richest man in the cemetery doesn't matter to me. Going to bed at night saying we've done something wonderful...that's what matters to me."

This perfectly encapsulates what should be the goal of Financial Planning ahead of death. In our role as Financial Planners, our clients are sometimes shocked to hear us encouraging them to spend their money, rather than zealously guard it ad infinitum.

The trouble is, how do we know with any certainty how much longer we have to live? All of our clients know their date of birth; none of them know their date of death.

If we knew precisely the date when we would shuffle off this mortal coil, Financial Planning would be a doddle. We could make some other assumptions about things like price inflation and then calculate a safe rate of withdrawal, letting our clients know precisely how much they could spend each month to ensure they ran out of money at precisely the same time they ran out of life.

As it is, with death dates being such an unknown quantity, we have to make some assumptions about that as well. We can start with average mortality (the Office for National Statistics - ONS publish some detailed figures on this) and then make allowances for family history, current state of health, smoker status and things like optimism.

Another approach is to simply assume you will live until your 100th birthday; unlikely but possible in this time of rapidly improving longevity.

Making an assumption about life expectancy which exceeds the average by a reasonable margin means your Financial Plan will err on the side of caution. You might not end up the richest man in the graveyard; you are at least able to understand what a safe level of additional expenditure in retirement looks like without running too high of a risk of running out of cash.

This could mean extra expenditure on you and your immediate family; boosting your lifestyle, experiencing more and generally living life to its fullest throughout your retirement, based on your available wealth.

This form of Financial Planning can also facilitate the sort of inter-generational wealth transfers we discussed earlier in this book, safe in the knowledge you can give capital to children or grandchildren without personally running out of money when you need it.

As well as making gifts to the next generation, Financial Planning and lifetime cash flow forecasting based on an assumed date of death can allow you to become more philanthropic. The ability to support favourite charities during your lifetime, rather than leaving a legacy on death, can be ultimately more satisfying, as you get to see the direct benefit of your donations.

Case Study – Being prepared

As they approached their final years, Joyce and Frank started making plans and important decisions. Having been financially self-sufficient their whole lives it was incredibly important to them not to be a burden on their two sons in the later stages of retirement.

Joyce had already arranged all of the details of her own funeral, but as she had never handled the household finances, Frank appointed us to work with the couple and their two sons to fully understand their finances. He was keen to ensure we could help handle the couple's affairs in the event of Frank's death.

Frank had organised his financial affairs so that the couple's investments were handled by a wealth manager he trusted to act in the best interests of his wife should he pre-decease her, as he candidly explained he expects to happen. He had documented all of his financial information, making sure everything is in order, in the full expectation that he will predecease Joyce.

As women have longer life expectancy than men, this belief is commonly held and usually proved accurate.

Joyce and Frank gained a great deal of peace of mind by sitting down with us as we were able to summarise all of their financial arrangements, giving them peace of mind that they understood their financial circumstances.

Handing over the management of investments to a Financial Planner they could trust and making detailed plans for Joyce's funeral gave them enormous peace of mind.

Frank was less fussed about planning the details for his own funeral, leaving this decision making to Joyce and trusting her judgement on these matters.

Expert view

Simon Ferrar is founder of Clandon Wood Natural Burial in the Surrey Hills. A builder by profession, Simon had the vision to create a natural burial ground after experiencing a relative's natural burial which took place in a farmer's field in Worcestershire.

This experience gave Simon the inspiration to create a sustainable and responsibly managed natural burial site in Surrey. Clandon Wood was born and has become the largest fully managed natural burial site in Surrey.

We spoke to Simon about dying and how the post-war generation are changing the institution of death, as they face up to this final stage of life.

Ready, Steady, Retire!: How did you get started with Clandon Wood?

Simon Ferrar: I came to natural burial through my aunt's funeral nine years ago, back in 2005. It was a very simple burial, consisting of a willow basket in a shallow grave in what was then a farmer's field in Worcestershire. It really was a light bulb moment for me. It was a beautiful simplicity.

I had no preconceptions at the time about burials or cremations. I just thought it was beautiful, and that's the way it should be done. I had it in my head ever since, for four or five years, until I found the land here at Clandon Wood in 2009. It took us two years through planning to be granted permission to create a burial ground here in the green belt on the edge of Guildford in Surrey.

We had our very first burial here in September 2012, I remember it very well. We had a total of nine burials in our first year. Then last year, 2013, the meadow developed and our buildings and our infrastructure were completed. We officially opened on Summer Solstice in June 2013. We have been going from strength to strength since then.

Ready, Steady, Retire!: What's the purpose of a natural burial ground?

Simon Ferrar: The environment, as you will have seen, has started to mature with the meadows. It will change year on year. Eventually both fields will have over 30 acres of wildflower meadow. Eventually they will be surrounded by oak, silver birch and lime. The creation of natural burial grounds really is about creating new environments, or improving, or looking after existing natural environments.

What we've done here at Clandon Wood is create a nature reserve. It's very young in its development. It's a nature reserve because a natural burial ground needs a reason to exist over and above just being a cemetery. The problems we've had in the past with traditional cemeteries, churchyards, and municipal cemeteries; once they're full they need maintaining. It costs money to maintain them, and that's all they can ever be.

In central London, for example, there's a huge problem with finding new burial space. The need now, for burials, means they're talking about lifting and lowering burial graves. Also, in certain London cemeteries they're actually flattening old gravestones, ones that are over 100 years old, flattening gravestones and then putting another six foot of soil on top.

I feel that a natural burial ground does away for the need of any of that need. What we're doing here, we're taking what was fallow land because this land had lain set aside for eight years, hadn't been planted. We have now created a nature reserve. When this land is full up, it is a nature reserve.

Ready, Steady, Retire!: How does natural burial differ from what we consider to be a traditional funeral or burial?

Simon Ferrar: From those very early stages when I went to my auntie's burial, back nine years ago now, it has become very important to me to see that the way that we look after our dead is now going back to what we regard, perhaps, as old days, but what I regard as tradition. The tradition that's accepted now, with the black hats and the undertakers, really probably only goes back 150, 200 years.

Within natural burial grounds, and the Association of Natural Burial Grounds, and the Natural Death Center who are the monitoring charity, we are not reinventing anything. This is what has been done for generations, probably for thousands of years. Families' members have died and the village takes care of it. The church, perhaps, might have taken care of it. It's all about the family.

This is what we're trying to bring back. We're trying to bring back the family involvement so that when someone dies, the family is there. Hopefully the person that has died has put plans in place about their wishes, their desires, about how they would like to die, how they would like to be treated when they are coming to the end of their life.

Ready, Steady, Retire!: How important is that family involvement?

Simon Ferrar: It can be very cathartic for a family. A lot of children don't want to accept their parents are going to die. If a parent can bring about the conversation before they're ill and before they're incompetent to actually write down their wishes, perhaps, it can help the family come to terms with the fact, yes, they are going to die. We all know, but people won't come to terms with it. They won't talk about it.

They come to terms with it, and also then start talking about the wishes, the desires, how they would like to be treated. Then the family can then accept and put into place the actions that they need to do when someone dies. If the family member wants to die at home, for example, then plans can be put into place so that's possible.

Ready, Steady, Retire!: When is the best time to start thinking about these end of life issues, such as funeral arrangements?

Simon Ferrar: The earlier you can start thinking about it, one, the more manageable it is from a financial point of view, and we have young families visiting here that are very early on in the family development.

They've been married. They've got young children. They've got a mortgage. They're starting to put the financial protection for their family in place, their life insurance in place, and the pension plans in place. Well, what's next? After the pension plan, really, is a funeral plan and death plans.

It might seem crazy at 30, 40, 50 years old, but the average age of the people that we've buried here is under 60. Yes, we have got 80 and 90 year olds, but the average age is probably under 60. That is quite something for people to think about.

Ready, Steady, Retire!: Death has always been considered something of a taboo. Is the post-war generation redefining death and becoming more comfortable when it comes to talking about dying?

Simon Ferrar: It has become slightly less of a taboo. I think there is still an awful lot of people that do not want to discuss the fact of their demise. But there are an awful lot more outlets for people to discuss openly, and in public a lot of ways with the Death Cafes, death salons, and Dying Awareness Week, for example.

There's a lot more information and discussion online. There's becoming a lot more television programs and documentaries done by the BBC and the mainstream filmmakers.

Ready, Steady, Retire!: Are there especially good places to have these conversations?

Simon Ferrar: I find that Clandon Wood, a natural burial ground, is a great venue for people to bring the subject of death and dying to the family, because people come out and they're walking through a nature reserve. They don't see a grave unless they walk right past one, a freshly dug one. If the grave is a year old then the meadow would have grown up through it anyway.

They feel comfortable here. Our office and reception is a comfortable place to be. It is an area that people recognize. There's a kitchen there. There's a sitting lounge, sitting area. The desk is at the back. We make people feel comfortable. When they walk in, you can physically see it, especially if it's a recent bereavement. You can physically see them relax. It's not threatening. There's nothing to worry about. It's not scary.

This environment makes it very easy to talk about. We do get people coming out looking. One, they don't know what it is. They pass on the roadside and come in curious. The others come in on purpose because they've seen me talking or presenting, and come and discuss it. There are others that have been diagnosed with a serious illness.

Ready, Steady, Retire!: How do conversations about dying tend to go?

Simon Ferrar: They are conversations that...they're obviously very earnest. Generally, the person who we're designing a funeral for, goes away with a sense of relief that they know where they're going to be. I have had families say to me, "Do you know what? Kind of, in a silly way, I'm looking forward to this, or looking forward to being here." That might seem a very, very simple thing to say, but if you imagine someone that has a terminal illness, it can make sense.

The particular gentleman that said that had had cancer for five years. He knew he was within his last six weeks of life. He wanted to put all his plans into place. He had his will written, he had labels on everything at home, who was going to have what. He had spoken to the family. Everyone knew what he wanted, his wishes, what his funeral would look like.

He had come out, chosen his plot. His wife has also chosen the plot next door to him. He came back to the office and said, "In a funny sort of way, I'm looking forward to being here." It's hugely humbling. It's a great honour to meet people like that that are facing up to the biggest unknown of their lives. That's part of the joy and reward that I get from doing this.

Ready, Steady, Retire!: How important is it to include your family in discussions about dying, what are effectively very personal decisions?

Simon Ferrar: It is a very good thing to talk to the family, and not just the children, but whoever it is that's involved with your will.

That includes who you select as your executors so that everybody is very well aware of who you've chosen and why you've chosen them, and if any of the family that are involved with the will have any issues with what you've decided, so that that can be discussed.

They can find out the reasons why you've decided to do what you have done. Once you've listened to what they've had to say, you might feel, "OK, yeah. I understand. Perhaps, we might need to alter that." When it comes to the time of your death, everybody is very well aware of what's been decided, why it's been decided, and then who is going to do the administration of the will.

Ready, Steady, Retire!: Is the Baby Boomer generation more likely to reject tradition and choose an approach which is more personal?

Simon Ferrar: I think from the Baby Boomer perspective, looking at the families we've had here, I would say...yeah, I would probably agree with that. The families that have had the traditional feel, the men in black, the black cars, the hearse, they have tended to be the pre-war generation. It is the younger members of the family who have kind of tempered that funeral, with a natural burial ground, so that the practical aspects of getting a body to a burial ground or to a crematorium, is tempered by a natural burial ending, whether it's a full body burial or a burial of ashes.

The traditional part begins and ends when the body gets delivered to the natural burial ground, for example, then the family takes over. There's been that discussion, hopefully. Most of the families here have generally had that discussion. The family then can have their input and their feel and make it personal for them, for Mom, Dad, or Nan and Grandad's funeral.

Ready, Steady, Retire!: How are funerals here financed? I assume that paying for the cost of a funeral is something we all need to consider?

Simon Ferrar: We offer funeral plans here. They're not a funeral plan that will divide it in various gold, silver, bronze, one, two, three levels. It is about what you want here. You decide. You come in here, decide what it is you want. If you want a horse and cart to the grave then you price that in. If you want a willow coffin, you price that in. If you want part of what we're calling a traditional funeral, such as the black hearse, you can have that as well. You price it all in.

That package, then, you just pay for that at today's prices. That goes into a trust fund. The provider of that, either us or a funeral arranger, will then pay for that funeral whenever it happens on the proceeds from that trust. That is part of the funeral plan. Also, from a point of view at Clandon Wood here, you can pre-purchase a plot. That can be done over a period of three years at no extra cost.

A basic plot here, at the moment, in 2014, is £1,070. Over three years I think that's something like £29 a month, or something like that. It's very affordable, and it does two things.

It is affordable so that you can pay for it and your family don't have to worry about it. Two, you don't have to worry about the fact that when you are going, the family are going to have to worry about what you want and having to pay for it. The time of a death is not the time to be making emotional decisions or a major financial decision about having to pay for a funeral.

If finances haven't been put in place, generally a funeral can be financed from the estate. They are funds that a solicitor or bank will pay before the estate's been sorted out.

Chapter Nine
Creating a Plan

Creating a Plan

"A big part of financial freedom is having your heart and mind free from worry about the what-ifs of life." - Suze Orman

For some soon-to-be retirees, the prospect of openly discussing their financial circumstances is not an idea that they relish. Whether it be a reluctance to discuss money issues generally or a belief in their own self-sufficiency, many people feel they can plan for their retirement alone.

In a recent survey, only 13% of over 45s said they would consult a financial adviser for guidance when making decisions about funding their care[52]. On a broader retirement planning level, an LV study found that only 29% had actually taken professional advice regarding their income options at retirement[53].

DIY retirement planning

Of those not yet retired, the same study found that only 12% were intending to speak to a professional adviser in the future. This growing trend for DIY retirement planning is of concern, given the general lack of awareness around retirement options LV identified.

For example, two-thirds of respondents didn't know that they could just take their pension commencement lump sum at retirement and leave the rest of their pension fund invested until they are ready to take an income.

It could be argued that many people won't have the tools to prepare themselves for retirement; a recent YouGov study found that 38% are already nervous about a shortage of funds and two thirds of respondents (66%) said that their priority is maintaining their current standard of living into retirement[54].

The complexity around pensions legislation and the constant changing of the rules keeps us as Financial Planners busy staying up to date! It is expecting a lot of someone without the technical expertise to keep abreast of all of the options open to them.

Arguably this problem of a lack of knowledge around investment and savings options is likely to worsen with the array of new pension investment and savings products likely to enter the market when the proposed pension reforms come into force in 2015.

Given that a third of those nearing retirement identified having enough money to live comfortably in retirement as the most important factor for them - only slightly behind health and well ahead of having a partner or rewarding family life - the need to understand your projected financial circumstances in retirement is critical.

Obviously, retirement income is the foundation stone of a successful retirement but this would be just one facet of retirement planning that a Financial Planner would consider.

The value of advice

Over the years various studies have proven financial advice to be beneficial for many people. Recent research from AXA shows that financial advice encourages people to save more for retirement and helps them to feel better prepared for their golden years[55]. When comparing the financial situations of consumers who have taken financial advice with those who haven't, some remarkable differences become clear:

- Savers who received advice benefit from an additional income of £3,654 every year of their retirement.

- 43% of UK savers approaching retirement increase their retirement savings levels by £98 a month as a direct result of taking financial advice, boosting their savings levels from £89 a month pre-advice to £187 post-advice.

- People who receive advice feel better prepared for their retirement than those who don't.

- 78% of advisers feel they can boost clients' retirement income if they seek advice 15 years before retirement, whereas only 28% of advisers think they can boost clients' retirement income if they seek advice at retirement.

So getting advice early can be incredibly beneficial to your income in retirement.

What's more, financial advice doesn't just prove its worth in the hard numbers. It also plays an important role in helping people understand their personal financial situation and how it fits into the wider financial environment of the national and global economy.

Needs at retirement

In our experience, those who do seek advice most frequently approach Planners with specific questions or issues to resolve, often based around financial products. Questions such as: "How and when should I draw my pensions?" often mask a lack of awareness about the concept and benefits of Financial Planning and the complexity of financial products available in modern markets.

Many Baby Boomers have amassed various pensions over their working life and are faced with complex decisions to make with regards to how to access those pensions. We do not believe, however, that product-related questions should be the first questions someone approaching retirement should ask.

A lifetime of retirement saving will not guarantee your comfort and security if you're tossing and turning through sleepless nights, unsure about the provisions you've made. At 3 a.m. it's easy to fret: 'I don't think we're organised', 'I'm sure we're missing something somewhere.' We call these your 3 a.m. moments.

For Baby Boomers who have often had varied career paths, compiling and combining retirement plans and benefits can be confusing.

Unlike previous generations who often worked for one employer and benefited from one final salary pension scheme, Boomers may have to combine a tangled mess of financial instruments: debt, final salary pensions, state pensions, personal pensions, and personal savings as well.

The Department of Work and Pensions calculates that 50-64 year olds have spent on average 13.9 years in their current employment, compared with 7.3 years for those aged 25-49, suggesting that this trend of complex and varied pension arrangements looks set to intensify with the second-wave of Boomers[56].

Trying to form a big picture of your financial situation can be daunting. A comprehensive Financial Plan should and will address these anxieties, bringing together all possible income streams, working through different "what if" scenarios and ensuring your retirement funds can support the lifestyle you intend to lead, whilst having the flexibility and responsiveness to react to unexpected events, good or bad.

Planning for the whole family

Many Boomers consider their personal circumstances and relationships to be an important part of their retirement planning. They recognize that they are fundamental in establishing a real sense of preparedness and peace of mind.

For older members of this generation, a key concern may be how their spouses, partners or extended families will cope financially after their death. As discussed in previous chapters, there has often been one individual within a couple who has "handled the money".

A genuine anxiety for some couples, with one spouse more financially organised and aware than the other, is the concern as to whether the surviving spouse will be able and prepared to proficiently handle the family finances. Such concerns and anxieties are important to address within the retirement planning process.

For Boomers who have had elderly parents predecease them, the struggles of probate alongside the financial re-organisation necessary after a family member's death can be especially apparent.

A thorough and comprehensive Financial Plan, formulated with expert advice and input - either from a Financial Planner or a free service - can help guarantee that both your needs and those of your loved ones are taken into account, to support you sufficiently through, and beyond, old age.

Having open discussions

Even once clear goals and needs in retirement have been identified, discussing them in depth openly is necessary to highlight any conflicts or disparities. It is surprisingly common to meet with a couple approaching retirement who have never held a frank and detailed discussion about what they envisage their retirement to look like, or what's important to each of them.

These discussions can sometimes best be facilitated by an independent third party who, with the experience and skills to be able to ask the right questions, at the right time, can help create a shared vision for the future for those embarking upon retirement.

The post-war generation, with an unparalleled period of longevity in front of them, must confront the challenge of planning and preparing for the later years in retirement, whilst still enjoying a high quality of life in their earlier retirement years. By doing this successfully they will be in a position to travel to exotic places, explore new hobbies, and give time and money back to their local communities - whatever is important to each and every person to feel fulfilled in retirement.

These choices must again be further balanced with other needs; perhaps a desire to support children or grandchildren financially as they attend university, or help younger generations find their first rung on the property ladder.

For any retiree, the complex needs of retirement are far greater than having simple questions about how best to access pensions answered. It is so important to explore your full range of needs, hopes, dreams, aspirations and demands to ensure the best possible outcome for you and your family.

Expert view

We interviewed John Perks, Managing Director of product provider LV= Retirement Solutions:

Ready, Steady, Retire!: Are Baby Boomers equipped to plan a retirement on their own?

John Perks: You can, but it's quite difficult. I think money spent on advice is proven to be worthwhile. People really do benefit from seeking out advice in some way. I think it's important for those approaching retirement to really understand their options and the implications of the choices they make, and talking to a Financial Planner is the most comprehensive way to do that.

Some research we did showed that only around 12% of people planned to use an adviser to plan for their retirement and the large majority were going to turn to different sources, such as family, friends, or the internet. That's quite a scary statistic. I would be more comfortable if people were really expertly well-prepared.

Ready, Steady, Retire!: What is needed to help Baby Boomers plan a successful retirement?

John Perks: When it comes to retirement decisions, education really is becoming more and more important, on so many levels. There's real enthusiasm from those approaching retirement because they've got a lot of ownership of how their future will look, and they know they can make choices that will improve their future.

On the flipside, there's also real fear that suddenly they've got this huge responsibility and they don't really know enough about this complex area to make informed decisions. More education is needed and that education needs to give people a thirst to then go on to seek advice as well.

What makes great Financial Planning?

The internationally recognised six step Financial Planning process is considered the gold standard approach for creating a holistic Financial Plan.

Consideration is given to all aspects of Financial Planning from investments to cash management, inflation to tax rate projections, health to life expectancy, tax planning to long term care planning, and from wills and trusts to charitable giving.

Before delving into the six step Financial Planning process and considering how this might work for you, it's important to establish whether the retiree and the planner can collaborate on creating a plan. Most financial planners will offer an initial consultation at their expense, which allows both parties to explore whether there is a good relationship fit, with no obligation for either side.

You will have an opportunity to explain what you are looking to achieve, whilst understanding what you can expect from working with the Financial Planner, what services they can provide, what value you will derive and what fees you will be charged.

Step 1: Establishing goals

If you decide to move forward in working with your chosen planner, he will then spend time at the first stage getting to know you and what's important to you. He will ask you a series of questions to uncover your goals, dreams and aspirations.

While this sounds simple, it can be quite complex, as retirees often have conflicting goals: a desire to live well in their early retirement years whilst being financially secure enough to obtain necessary care in their later years.

These goals should be set for the short, medium and long term, which further complicates the process, as people tend to end up with many goals that require planning for individually, within one holistic Financial Plan.

More importantly, a thorough understanding of goals should extend beyond pure financial targets; it's important that you use this time to really think about how you may want to spend each and every day. These are the types of questions you should ask yourself:

- What's important to me?

- Who do I want to spend time with?

- What do I want to spend time doing?

For many people who have never really had the chance to explore these kinds of ambitions, this stage of the Financial Planning process can be truly transformative.

Step 2: Current financial circumstances

Having established what you want to work towards (your planning objectives) your planner will analyse and evaluate your current financial circumstances. This includes collating a picture of your current assets and liabilities, your current and projected income and expenditure, including when you expect to receive your state pension and what level of income that will deliver to you.

At this stage, your Financial Planner will begin to consider how the assets may be utilised to deliver against your identified planning goals.

Step 3: Analyse your existing plans

Now, the focus is upon analysing your existing plans and what they could deliver to you, alongside your assets and liabilities. The very nature of the financial services industry makes this process so complex that a professional is often needed to help unravel and interpret the jargon, whilst taking account of the current tax regulations.

Fundamental to this understanding is creating a cash flow model that projects your anticipated incomings and outgoings for your lifetime. Lifetime cash flow modelling allows someone to plan for several possible scenarios.

In an ideal world, most retirees would want to spend their last penny on their very last day on earth, but planning that efficiently is difficult for even the most seasoned Financial Planner. By building different "what-if" scenarios into your plan, you can consider the effects on you and your security.

Many of our retired clients are keen to support their children or grandchildren, so in that case we suggest asking questions such as:

- Well, what if we give our grandchildren £20,000 a year for the next 3 years?

- What if we pay their tuition fees?

- What if we help our children clear their debts?

- What if we help them get on the property ladder?

Asking yourself these questions will enable you to compare outcomes in a complete and holistic way.

Planning for financial market volatility is also a key component. You should consider answers to the following questions:

- What if we had another 2008-type financial crisis, what impact does that have on our wealth?

- When are we going to run out of money?

Taking into account all assets and liabilities, risk factors, and dreams and aspirations can offer essential insight. By planning for many and varied scenarios, you can interact and engage with your Plan to understand it fully.

Step 4: Developing your Financial Plan.

This consists of a summary of recommendations which will take you towards the achievement of your goals, essentially a 'route map' to help you manage your wealth in order to achieve what's important to you. This is built following discussions around your lifetime cash flow and will be your ongoing strategy in order to meet your most important goals.

Step 5: Implement the recommendations

This step involves implementing your financial planning recommendations and making the changes identified to realise your goals. This may involve buying financial products such as ISAs or pensions, or it may involve drawing down on your existing pensions, or structuring your portfolio in a different way. Whatever the recommendations, your Financial Planner can advise on how to bring your plan to fruition.

Step 6: Review regularly

The sixth step of the Financial Planning process is a commitment to periodic review and revaluation. Without the final step of the process your Financial Plan can become meaningless.

Circumstances change regularly, so these changes must be incorporated in to your cash flow and your Financial Plan to ensure you are not only working towards the right goals, but are still on track to achieve them.

What's Financial Life Planning?

Financial Life Planning recognises the link between money and the meaning of your life. It takes a comprehensive view of what you truly value, helps you identify your life goals and plan financially to achieve them.

In comparison to the approach outlined above, a Financial Planner trained in Financial Life Planning will spend a significantly longer amount of time at step one asking you in-depth questions about what's truly important to you.

No mention is usually made of money until your personal goals, priorities and ambitions have been explored in depth.

A Financial Life Planner will then go on to follow the rest of the six step Financial Planning process as all other Financial Planners would, but may have uncovered deeper dreams and desires than Planners not trained in the Financial Life Planning approach.

What's in a name?

We have talked at length about Financial Planners, but what exactly is one?

A Financial Planner is not an over-eager IFA (Independent Financial Adviser) trying to sell a product to make end-of-month quotas. A Financial Planner provides crucial support in the transition to retirement, asking the right questions to make the transition a smooth and fulfilling one.

Planning how you want to live in retirement should be the starting point before you even discuss the funds you have available to support your later years.

To plan a fulfilling retirement is to decide exactly what you want to do with the rest of your years, then making sure your finances can support those aspirations.

By planning your finances to meet your goals with the help of a highly qualified Financial Planning professional you will have much greater confidence of where you are going in life, reduce your stress levels and be able to enjoy life more. Crucially, you will gain peace of mind through knowing that you're on track to achieve what's important to you and your family.

Although it can be tempting to undertake this planning alone, an objective third-party view is an essential part of a Financial Planner's service, as often we, and even our most trusted friends and family lack the specific knowledge, planning expertise, and discipline to do this on our own.

A Financial Planner can give informed advice about specific financial products if needed, but more importantly, a Financial Planner will commit to an ongoing process - the six step process outlined above - to help you make smart choices about money.

This process can help you achieve the financial and life goals you have set for yourself in retirement and later life, using a far more integrated and holistic system than just buying financial products.

What to look for in a Financial Planner

Years have passed since the credit crunch crisis, when the inadequacies of some firms and individuals within the financial services industry were exposed.

Those delivering advice today are subject to significantly higher expectations in terms of minimum qualifications and fiduciary responsibility. Trustworthiness, integrity and accountability are key attributes that you must seek to be satisfied by your retirement planning partner.

A great starting point is to ensure your planner holds a Certified Financial Planner qualification, usually designated CFP. A CFP certification is the only globally recognised mark of professionalism for Financial Planners.

A CFP professional will have had to demonstrate that he or she can follow a rigorous process for delivering financial advice which allows them to deliver and develop a well-rounded Financial Plan for anyone entering or enjoying their retirement.

In essence they will employ the six step Financial Planning process discussed earlier. They have the skills and experience to help you thoroughly and effectively review all of your options so that you can make informed decisions about what you want from all aspects of life, both now and in the future.

Check that any financial adviser you're considering has at least a 'Level 4' qualification. This is the minimum qualification the industry regulator, the Financial Conduct Authority (FCA), says all IFAs in Britain must hold.

However, to ensure you find a Financial Planner with the level of knowledge and expertise you deserve, search for someone who has achieved Chartered status. Chartered or Certified (as discussed above)

Planners have achieved a 'Level 6' qualification. They have been examined in the technical detail not only of financial advice, but also the creation and implementation of a Financial Plan.

Furthermore, if someone has invested the time and energy to become both a Chartered Financial Planner (through the Chartered Insurance Institute) and a Certified Financial Planner (through the Institute of Financial Planning) they are pretty serious about being at the top of their profession by virtue of education and qualifications.

These standards are international, and exceptional Financial Planners can be found all over the world.

Some British planners may reference a British Standard, BS ISO 22222. This standard requires that planners adhere to a similarly holistic Financial Planning process, but also demonstrate commitment and dedication to continual improvement and ensure client satisfaction is at the core of the business culture.

Planners who hold ISO 22222, and firms that hold British Standard BS 8577, are subject to ongoing external assessment not only of their services, but of their overall practice.

Additionally, firms that have gone one step further and become an Accredited Financial Planning Firm™ have been independently assessed as meeting the highest standards of service, delivered with the utmost care and ethical practice by highly qualified individuals.

All planners should agree a fee with you for the services they will provide. Ask about the fee structure and service you will receive up front. If you want to ensure you get a truly unbiased recommendation then make sure your Financial Planner is genuinely independent, meaning he can make a recommendation from the whole of the market, and thus the most suitable recommendation for you.

Finding a planner

Finding a Financial Planner takes time and energy. The best starting point for finding a Certified Financial Planner is through the Institute of Financial Planning. Their website at www.financialplanning.org.uk/wayfinder offers tools for searching by postcode, and can give information about Financial Planners in your area and their firms.

To find a Chartered Financial Planner check out the Chartered Insurance Institute's website www.cii.co.uk.

You may also consider getting recommendations from people who you think are smart with their money.

Failing that, there are independent organisations established for the sole purpose of helping individuals find the right Financial Planner for them.

Unbiased.co.uk is the leading such UK-based website which only lists independent financial advisers and uses advanced search tools so you can select only Chartered Financial Planners, Accredited Financial Planning Firms™, or those with specific types of experience.

Questions to ask your Financial Planner

Once you have created a shortlist of Financial Planners you would consider working with, don't hesitate in contacting each one and asking some key questions about them, their business, their experience, and their approach. After all, most planners will offer an initial consultation at their expense, so take the time to ensure you choose the right planner for you.

Below are some of the questions you may wish to ask, and the reasons why:

1. What qualifications do you have? Look for Chartered and / or Certified to ensure they are at the top of their profession.

2. What experience do you have of working with people like me? Can they demonstrate they understand your needs by virtue of experience and specialisation?

3. What is your approach to Financial Planning? Do they adhere to the six step process?

4. How will I pay for your services? Will you have the opportunity of receiving the service, and appreciating the benefits, before you pay?

5. What are your fees? Make sure their fee structure is transparent and you understand what you will pay and when.

6. How often will we meet? Is there an ongoing service, after the initial advice? This can be crucial to help stick to and update your plan.

Going it alone

For Boomers with the confidence, expertise and discipline to develop their own comprehensive retirement plan, there are reputable free advice services to turn to when in doubt.

The government-run Money Advice Service is an independently run service set up by the UK Government to answer questions about money management honestly and impartially. Offering support through face-to-face meetings, chats online or over the phone, or through print and digital resources available through their website, the Money Advice Service offers guidance on debt management, pension planning, tips for maximising your savings and investment, and clear advice on tax issues surrounding death and inheritance.

While freely available Financial Planning tools provide high-quality advice and information, remember that a free service may not be able to explore any personal issues in the same depth as a planner face to face.

If you elect to use one, it is important to approach your retirement planning by taking the time and effort to consider your needs and circumstances in retirement, and take a rigorous approach when considering possible scenarios for the future.

Top websites for money guidance

Below is a list of some of the most popular websites you may wish to consult for information, guidance and opinion if you decide to take the DIY approach to retirement planning:

Moneysavingexpert.co.uk

Motleyfool.co.uk

Whichmoney.co.uk

Financialplanning.org.uk/wayfinder

Moneyadviceservice.org.uk

Thisismoney.co.uk

Considerations for your retirement plan

As discussed, a clear and comprehensive approach to retirement is essential to guarantee your happiness, fulfilment and security. Below are some important considerations for how you approach planning for retirement - whether you choose to work with a professional or 'go it alone':

- **Plan early:** The evidence shows that planning early can result in a more financially successful retirement than leaving it to the last minute. So start thinking about, planning for and funding your retirement as early as you can.

- **Talk about it:** Your retirement will affect both you and your family, so discussing your plans for retirement with loved ones, especially your spouse, is essential, both for financial reasons and as an important sounding board for your ambitions for retirement. Establish the kinds of relationships you hope to maintain or build with your family to help you feel involved and engaged, for example, in your children and grandchildren's lives.

- **Work out what's important to you:** Discussing your goals and priorities and working out firmly what they are and why they are important is crucial. Your family can offer advice, but so can friends, colleagues, and Financial Planners. Solicit a wide range of opinions from every facet of your life to help find ways to continue the activities and involvements that are already important to you. Perhaps find options for pursuing new activities - a new volunteer placement, a local community group, or an exotic vacation to an unknown island.

  Take this time in retirement to define or redefine yourself and explore how you will continue that identity. Retirement is a unique opportunity to focus upon yourself and your personal fulfilment.

- **Work out your finances:** With your clearly established goals in mind, you are in a powerful position to examine your personal finances in detail and decide whether you are financially able to do all the things you would like or need to do at varying stages of retirement. Do not shy away from identifying shortfalls. An early identification can give greater options for making up the desired income, through new commercial ventures, flexible work opportunities or structuring your assets differently.

Calculating your income needs in the different stages of retirement is essential. You may need greater resources in the early years, less once you have completed everything on your "bucket list", and then more once again if you need care in later life.

Estimating the impact of inflation upon your income needs is of course key to these calculations. Try calculating your income less tax - both for now and for future points during your retirement. It may be that you are not eligible to receive your state pension for another five years, so your income stream will be healthier from that point.

Your income may be from various sources such as state pensions, occupational pensions, private pensions, annuities, dividends, other benefits and interest from savings or investments.

It is also important to calculate your expenditure - again, both current and projected expenses at different points of your retirement. This could include transport, council tax, utility bills, insurance premiums, telephone bills, holidays, gifts for birthdays and Christmas, regular payments to family members, socialising, entertaining and club subscriptions or hobbies.

Deducting your annual current and projected expenditure from your incomes will give you a quick overview of your ongoing financial health, and help flag any future shortfalls that you will need to plan for.

- **Calculate your net worth:** This exercise will give you an idea whether you are likely to face an Inheritance Tax liability:

    - Start by totting up your assets. Include your property, your investments, your savings and the value of your pension plans.

    - Deduct your liabilities, which may include mortgages, credit card debts, loans and overdrafts.

In our experience, people who keep track of what they spend find this to be a fantastic tool to enable financial success.

Putting aside, or earmarking, funds for short, medium and long term plans is a great way of making sure these plans actually happen. Furthermore, keeping money aside for unexpected events is critical to the success of any plan. In our experience, the financially well organised have a significantly less stressful life!

Plan for passing on your wealth

It is important to maintain clear communication with family and friends to ensure not only that wealth and assets are transferred efficiently, but also that your wishes are understood and respected. Planning for life's later stages will involve some consideration of how your wealth is to be passed on in the event of your death.

Unpleasant as it may be, a full plan for retirement should explore how and when your assets can be best passed on to your loved ones in an efficient and effective way.

First and foremost, make a will and take advice on legacy planning to ensure your wealth is passed on as tax efficiently as possible. The earlier you plan for this, the better, as some strategies are best implemented whilst you are still fit and active - if funds allow.

Discussing your end-of-life wishes with your family is essential to your long-term peace of mind in ensuring your wishes are respected, as we discussed in chapter eight. You may be surprised at how important close family find it to know how their loved ones want to end their days and have their wealth distributed. You can bring enormous peace of mind not only to yourself, but those you care most about, by planning for when you're gone.

Don't let your plan gather dust

Once you've created a plan of how you want to live in retirement, don't disregard it, never to be seen again.

Revisit your plan at least once a year, see what's changed that could throw you off track to doing all the things that are important to you, and update your plan if needs be. This may be changes to your income or expenditure, the illness or death of a loved one or an unexpected windfall or expense. A plan is an evolving tool that needs to respond to your ever-changing circumstances and needs.

In conclusion

The rigorous and complex process of retirement planning can be accomplished alone. Using a Financial Planner is not for everyone, and freely available resources, including published books and impartial websites, provide extremely good quality information and support in creating a plan for your retirement.

For others, the involvement of an objective third party in the planning process can be extremely beneficial. As planners sift through details and ask questions you may not have thought of, they can often discover hopes and needs in retirement that you may not have considered yourself, and have experience exploring the financial arrangements needed to support them.

An in-depth analysis of your hopes for retirement, drafting a plan, periodic review and systematic implementation can be essential to providing peace of mind, and the comfort, security and empowerment that Boomers crave - and deserve - in retirement. A Planner's commitment can help foster strong decision making and impart a much-craved sense of true freedom in retirement.

But take time to find the right planner for you, as this person could be helping you make some of the most important financial decisions of your life.

What a robust financial plan really allows retirees to do is to get on with living a fulfilling retirement - educating yourself, enjoying new hobbies, spending time with family, volunteering in the local community - safe in the knowledge that your 3 a.m. moments have been addressed.

You know that your finances support you doing all of the things that make you fulfilled. You know you have a plan if one of you needs to go into care, or if one of you dies then your wealth transfer plan is clearly mapped out, is understood by your loved ones, and is as tax efficient as possible.

So when those events arise - as one or more undoubtedly will during any 20-30 year retirement - you can just pull your plan out of the drawer and say 'We know what to do about that", instead of worrying and not being able to enjoy, what for many Boomers is proving to be, a hugely rewarding second act.

References

References

1 House of Commons Library Research, The Ageing Population, (2010, UK)

2 Odgers Bendtston, After The Baby Boomers, (2012, London, UK)

3 Department for Communities and Local Government Labour Force Survey (April

2013)

4 McVeigh, Tracy, Divorcing baby boomers seize the moment to go it alone, The Observer (June 2013)

5 House of Commons Library Research, The Ageing Population, (2010, UK)

6 British Medical Association, Captivating Vision Care, Riley (1998, UK)

7 "Retire to Sussex!", Sussex Council Publication, via the archives of the London Transport Museum

8 Age UK, "Paying for Permanent Residential Care", (2014, UK)

9 Office for National Statistics, Life Expectancy at Birth and Age 65: 2008-2010, (2010, UK)

10 Centre for Disease Control and Prevention, "Healthy Ageing", (2011, USA)

11 Royal College of Psychiatrists, "Depression and Anxiety in Older People", (August 2014, UK)

12 Consumers, Saving and Investing, UK, January 2014; GMI/Mintel. Study of 2,000 internet users aged > 18

13 GMI/Mintel, Consumers, Saving and Investing, UK, January 2014; Study of 2,000 internet users aged > 18, (January 2014, UK)

14 The Changing Face of Retirement - Future Patterns of Work, Health, Care and Income among the Older Population, Institute of Fiscal Studies (2014)

15 The Prince's Trust Initiative for Mature Enterprise (September 2014)

16 Office for National Statistics (October 2014)

17 Wittenberg et al., Projections of Demand for and Cost of Social Care For Older People in England, (London, UK, 2011)

18 NESTA, 'Preparing for Ageing', (UK, 2009)19 Institute of Fiscal Studies, The Changing Face of Retirement, Future Patterns of Work, Health, Care and Income among the Older Population (UK, 2014)

20 Aviva Real Retirement Report (UK, 2013)

21 House of Lords, Public Service and Demographic Change Committee, 'Ready for Ageing? (UK, 2013).

22 Cameron, David, 'Older People Manifesto' (UK, 2010)

23 House of Lords, Public Service and Demographic Change Committee, 'Ready for Ageing?' (UK, 2013).

24 Age UK, Challenges of an Ageing Population, (April 2013, UK)

25 Metlife, The 2011 Metlife Study of the American Dream, (USA, November 2011)

26 Age UK, Challenges of an Ageing Population, (April 2013, UK)

27 Anthony, Mitch, The New Retirementality: Planning Your Life and Living Your Dreams at Any Age you Want, (USA, 2008)

28 YouGov, Retirement Planning 2011, (June 2011, UK)

29 Institute of Fiscal Studies, The Changing Face of Retirement: Future Patterns of Work, Health, Care and Income Among the Older Population, (June 2014, UK)

30 Department of Work and Pensions, Older Workers Statistical Information Booklet, (UK, 2012)

31 Institute of Fiscal Studies, The Changing Face of Retirement: Future Patterns of Work, Health, Care and Income Among the Older Population, (June 2014, UK)

32 Institute of Fiscal Studies, The Changing Face of Retirement: Future Patterns of Work, Health, Care and Income Among the Older Population, (June 2014, UK)

33 ResPublica, Age of Opportunity: Older People, Volunteering and The Big Society, (April 2011, UK)

34 PriceWaterhouseCopper, How will the Wealth of the Baby Bust Generation compare to that of the Baby Boomers?, (2012, UK)

35 King, Martin "30m Adults Have Not Made a Will", The Guardian, October 23rd, 2010

36 Age UK, Later Life in the United Kingdom (UK, 2014)

37 Harries, E & de Las Casas, L, 'Who will love me, when I'm 64?' (UK, 2013)

38 Bingham, J, The Telegraph, 'Til retirement us do part: 'silver splitter' divorces up by three quarters in a generation' (UK, 2013)

39 Office for National Statistics, Divorces in England and Wales (UK, 2013)

40 Daily Mail, 'Silver splitters: Growing number of elderly people are divorcing to live alone as they hit retirement' (UK, 2013)

41 Maxfield, J, The Motley Fool, Social Security: Why Taking Benefits at 62 Is Smarter Than You Think (US, 2014)

42 Harvard Medical School, Marriage and men's health (US, 2010)

43 Cacioppo, J, 'Loneliness', University of Chicago (US, 2014)

44 Institute of Public Policy Research, The Condition of Britain (UK, 2014)

45 ESRC Centre for Population Change, University of Southampton (UK, 2013)

46 Carers UK, Supporting employees who are caring for someone with dementia (UK, 2014)

47 Alzheimer's Society, The progression of Alzheimer's disease and other dementias (US, 2011)

48 Alzheimer's Society, Dementia 2013 Infographic (UK, 2013)

49 Kings College London & the London School of Economics, Dementia UK The Full Report (UK, 2007)

50 Roberts, M, BBC, Unhealthy Britain: nation's five big killers (UK, 2013)

51 Demos Commission on Residential Care (UK, 2014)

52 Partnership, Third Care Index Report 2014-15, (July 2014, UK)

53 Liverpool Victoria, State of Retirement Report 2014, (April 2014, UK)

54 YouGov Plc. Total sample size was 2,532 adults. Fieldwork was undertaken between 15 - 16 April 2014. The survey was carried out online. The figures have been weighted and are representative of all UK adults (aged 18+).

55 AXA, The Value of Advice Report (2014)

56 Office of National Statistics, Labour Force Survey, Q2 2011, (August 2011, UK)